JJ0645644

Why I
Hate the
Republicans

Why I Hate the Republicans

RANDY HOWE

The Lyons Press

Guilford, Connecticut
An imprint of The Globe Pequot Press

Copyright © 2004 by Randy Howe

ALL RIGHTS RESERVED. No part of this book may be reproduced or transmitted in any form by any means, electronic or mechanical, including photocopying and recording, or by any information storage and retrieval system, except as may be expressly permitted in writing from the publisher. Requests for permission should be addressed to The Lyons Press, Attn: Rights and Permissions Department, P.O. Box 480, Guilford, CT 06437.

The Lyons Press is an imprint of The Globe Pequot Press.

10 9 8 7 6 5 4 3 2 1

Designed by Heather Kern

Printed in the United States of America

ISBN 1-59228-437-X

Library of Congress Cataloging-in-Publication Data is available on file.

Dedication

To Chris Kuebler

If a book is constructed like a house, then its foundation has to be research. Among the sources I hoped to tap for this project was the nation's think tanks. There are a myriad of organizations that fall under this categorization, all dedicated to the collection, analysis, and dissemination of information. Some have a conservative agenda while others are more liberal. By interviewing the fine minds gathered therein, the number crunchers and policy paper writers, I hoped to be able to make available to you, the reader, the most up-to-date data possible.

Although I received tremendous support from several liberal think tanks, I did not hear back from any of the conservative. The Brookings Institute could not be bothered. They are apparently hard at work maintaining Colin Powell's rep as an African-American. (One outside source claims they are currently funding experiments in pigment transplantation, using Michael Jackson's cryogenically frozen skin cells.) The Heritage Foundation switched to an unlisted number after my seventh message. Each was longer than the last, my final diatribe likely to haunt me should I ever decide to run for office . . . I sent flowers to The National Center for Public Policy Research, but they were returned. Unopened but wilted from the stagnant air in their Capitol Street office. Not one of these conservative think tanks was kind enough to return my calls, emails, faxes, or smoke signals. In hindsight, I should've waited until I was in the belly of the beast to mention the name of the book—Trojan Horse them with a blue blazer and penny loafers.

Despite these minor setbacks, my research was extensive. So, rather than listing all of the agreeable sources, I have chosen instead to inform you, the reader, as to who is *not* included. Marketing suggested this would be more appealing anyway. That being said, congratulations; you now hold in your hand a book that was not influenced by: The Brooks Brothers Institute; The Spiro Agnew Center for Fiscal Integrity; The KKK Konsortium[1]; The Pocket Protector Perspective; Texans Against Taxes; Polemic Prodigies for Probity in Public Policy; The Mercedes, Benz, and Beemer Brotherhood; The Deport George Soros Society; The CommonWealth Collection; Rightgrrrl; The American Minority Fellowship[2]; and The Opposite of Progressive Policy Institute.

Despite the noncompliance of these privately funded organizations, hours of research went into *Why I Hate the Republicans*. Because this is a book about politics and politicians, all manner of spin doctoring, poetic license, and the gerrymandering of the truth have been employed—this, in an effort to fill in the blanks. The way Republicans withhold information, we have no choice but to root around and draw our own conclusions.

That being said, caveat emptor. Caveat Fat Cat.

---

[1] In conjunction with the Bob Jones University Distance Learning Program.

[2] No, not *those* kinds of minorities. Think not of kibbutz, Kwanzaa, or crossing the border, but of the 1 percent of the population that controls 40 percent of the wealth.

Certainly right now the conservative right does a much better job of feeding the media beast facts and arguments that make their case. On the progressive side of the aisle, we've been asleep at the wheel.
—Joe Lockhart

Rather than sending Americans to Mars or the moon right now, these people would be better off trying to figure out how to get Americans back from Iraq.
—John Kerry

I thought a hanging chad was what Bob Dole had before Viagra.
—Rep. Martin Frost (R-TX)

All animals are equal but some are more equal than others.
—George Orwell

Contents

Why I Hate the Republicans

All conservatives are such from personal defects. They have been effeminated by position or nature, born halt and blind, through luxury of their parents, and can only, like invalids, act on the defensive.
—Ralph Waldo Emerson

Bible thumping, radioactive dumping, responsibility punting, cheap oil hunting, defense spending, truth bending, currency conserving, silver-spoon undeserving, nepotism embracing, voting record about-facing, "the Fifth" pleading, hearts not bleeding, homosexual bashing, Third World smashing, talk radio calling, illegal arms hauling, golf club swinging, holy Gospel singing, CIA leaking, double talk speaking, fighter plane riding, morals and ethics sliding, law unabiding, military record hiding, civil rights chiding, censorship priding, and xenophobic siding doo doo heads. Big stinky *Elephas maximus* dung heads! That's what I think of when I think of the Republican Party.

This little book you hold in your hands is my answer to the conservative media, breastfed with statistics and p.r. propaganda from all of those conservative think tanks. It is my response to the ultra-conservatives who get all uppity when their transgressions qualify as "All the news that's fit to print." The truth hurts like a spanking, but it's time we made a few of these Grand Old Partiers drop trow; them and their loud-as-Limbaugh mouthpieces.

> In Britain, politicians who openly discuss their spirituality are about as welcome as Jehovah's Witnesses on the doorstep.
> —Gavin Esler

Abraham Lincoln was paraphrasing the Bible when he said, "A house divided against itself cannot stand." It was on those wings that the Republican Party rose to prominence. But before we get too caught up in angelic imagery, it's important to note that God does not have a seat reserved at our democratic table. No one has a guaranteed seat in our government—divine rights went out with King George. To get a spot at the table, you must *earn* it. Again and again and again. That's one of the wonderful things about democracy. Besides, as the Constitution plainly states, religion should be a private affair. Separate. There's nothing wrong with practicing your faith, just not on C-SPAN.

I can't decide what would tick God off more: knowing that felons in shoulder pads thank Him after demolishing the opposing quarterback or that His name appears on U.S. currency. If anything angers God, it's probably that a political party has the nerve to try and patent His name. That, in supposedly doing His good work, they are attempting to monopolize Him. And where is the Her in all this?

The Republican Party is also doing their darnedest to corner the market on the red, white, and blue. A house is not a home, just as nationalism isn't patriotism. The former is cold and blind; the latter is open and warm. I love my country enough to never, ever burn the flag, but also enough to protect the right of free speech.[3] And no matter what those Republican talking heads say, I like that the U.S. has no official language. Those GOP-inclined talk show hosts should

---

[3] If King George II was up on his American history, he'd know that the constitutional amendments are for affirming individual rights, not taking them away.

feel free to spout off in English, Spanish, even French! Just so long as the rights guaranteed us in the Constitution are protected. And the moment they even *suggest* adding amendments like a ban on gay marriage is the moment we start talking about eighty-sixing the right to bear arms. How do you think they'll like that trade-off?[4] We could call the movement "Gays for Guns," but that would probably be too confusing for the NRA.

I was born on the wrong side of the tracks, but the flags we waved were no different from those on the right side of the tracks. I was fortunate enough to have two parents at home to keep me . . . on track. They worked all week and then fixed up our handyman's special on the weekends. They busted hump to make a better life for my brother and me; to turn a house into a home. It's a cop-out and the most egregious of generalizations to think of poverty as being like a sexually transmitted disease. Wealth is a reference back to the days of divine right; nine times out of ten it's the result of winning the loin fruit lottery. And the sooner Republicans recognize the difference between work ethic and birth right the better. Poverty is rarely the result of a choice and it certainly isn't curable with penicillin or abstinence. Being working-class is not morally reprehensible.

> It's a moronarchy.
> —Imus, describing King George II's presidency

> We who are liberal and progressive know that the poor are our equals in every sense except that of being equal to us.
> —Lionel Trilling

We were not wealthy people—not by the standards of New York suburban living—but we were also never hungry or homeless. I wasn't born a crack baby and neither were my friends; those born in the same

5

---

[4] No more hunting trips for Scalia and Cheney. They'll have to take up bowling!

Money is better than poverty, if only for financial reasons.
—Woody Allen

town or those I eventually befriended in high school—from a neighboring town whose real estate values screamed "right side of the tracks"! I still love these friends dearly and am happy to say that, despite their silver sporks, none of them grew up to be like Randolph and Mortimer. They are not greedy adulterers who spend their time mixing martinis and laughing like Dr. Evil. They aren't hell-bent on accruing all they can by age forty and they aren't graduates of the "kid with the most toys wins" school of thought. But all too often they vote for those who are.

Many of my friends, high school and otherwise, voted for Bush-Cheney, and I don't know if I'll ever forgive them. This has made life somewhat awkward, as my wife is one of them. I am a teacher, and Dubya has decided to make education one of his platform issues, so let's look at our schools as a means of illustrating the error of their ways. (If you find me in Chateau BowWow tomorrow morning, you'll know why.)

Friends, family, countrymen, wife . . . we are currently too consumed with having our kids score five points higher on THE BIG TEST. Even more disturbing than the agenda of the GOP God Squad is what is happening in our schools. Violent kindergarteners, the loss of extracurricular programs, increased drop-out rates . . . And

I hate ingratitude more in a man than lying, vainness, babbling, drunkenness, or any taint of vice whose strong corruption inhabits our frail blood.
—William Shakespeare

really, is the answer to childhood obesity to take away recess? In teaching, we try to model for our students how we want them to complete a task. King George II hasn't modeled accountability in the least. Not in his budgets and not in being honest about Iraq. He

> All our children ought to be allowed a stake in the enormous riches of America.
> —Jonathan Kozol

certainly hasn't modeled following through with his "No Child Left Behind" legislation. Not with one-third of the funding still lost in translation. There must have been some heavy snow the day he mailed out those "NCLB" checks. You can expect a "leak" regarding the offending postal employee any day now . . .

King George II is interested in numbers like test scores, but uninterested in discussing numbers preceded by a dollar sign. He has proven this in areas other than education, but based on the example of "NCLB" alone, you can make a pretty good argument against him and his fellow fat-cat Republicans. The time has come to vote your conscience, friends, family, countrymen . . . wife! The time has come for simple math. I start not with sixty-five, but with fifty-five, the new and improved passing score in this age of accountability![5] Now that's what I call raising the bar . . .

Fifty-five is not just slightly better than half the questions right; it is a speed limit ignored; the age when

> He did not just break the spirit of his promises . . . He broke the obligations of the federal government.
> —Senator Dick Gephardt, referring to insufficient funding for "NCLB"

---

[5] One year in New York, too many kids failed their Regents exams, so the passing grade was dropped to 55 percent (which must be good if a 25 percent was enough to get King George II into the Texas Air National Guard!).

7

you weigh the benefits of the senior citizen discount against getting old. It's a big steel drum used to hold toxic waste; a local cable access channel; the number of words allowed in the world's shortest short story contest. Fifty-five is the number of cards in the "Iraq's Most Wanted" deck. Sometimes, it's even a passing grade: fifty-four and you don't get that diploma. And finally, in 2004, election #55 pits Bush #43 against Heinz #57.[6]

The Republican Party celebrates its 150th anniversary in 2004, too. Although the GOP did begin in grand style, complete with ethical behavior and a rock-steady platform, the men they've ushered into the Oval Office have, by and large, been a disappointment. The trend continues as the puppet masters prop up the crowned prince of Kennebunkport, settling, yet again, for the not-so grand.

Every day, I cross over to the wrong side of the tracks in order to teach. I'm greeted by a sign proclaiming New Haven as the birthplace of George W. Bush. And because of his vast intellect, his mastery of conversational English, and the fact that his father was an alumnus, the crowned prince also went to college here. Dental records prove he drank lots of beer and ate lots of apizza; one class-mate even recalls seeing him at matriculation.

These days, there is a conservative movement in many of the nation's colleges and universities. The GOP has a long line of re-cruits pouring forth, like water from the well. For example, the College Republicans at Roger Williams University recently sunk to a new level of insensitive snideness. A "whites only" scholarship is being offered by these young Republicans. Jason Mattera defended the notion as their protest against affirmative action. Across the campus, there are students who have benefited from such scholarships, but Materra doesn't much care how they feel. Odd, too, considering

---

[6] Interestingly enough, both George W. Bush and John Kerry are Skull and Bones men from Yale University.

he is of Puerto Rican descent and receiving $5,000 a year through a "minorities only" scholarship. The kid definitely has a future with the GOP.

Conservative talk shows keep priming the pump and prompting people like this to action, so I'm here to draw some

A conservative is someone who makes no changes and consults his grandmother when in doubt.
—Woodrow Wilson, 28th president of the United States of America

water for the liberals. I love politics, I love my country, but I hate that the Republicans have the upper hand right now (especially after reading about that smug little hypocrite in Rhode Island).

Elephas maximus has grown fat over the years; gluttonous with wealth while his memory has been laid to waste by indifference. It's as if Reagan's Alzheimer's is contagious; as addictive as William J. Bennett's gambling or Rush Limbaugh's OxyContin. I am not one to rush to judgment, but Rush has had no heart in the past, so I don't feel compelled to show him any forgiveness. I am a spiritual person, but not religious in that turn-the-other-cheek, by-the-book kind of way. Harsh words should come back to bite.

Republicans like Rush thrive on conflict. Theirs and the nation's. If we are going to pretend that there must always be a cold war and if we are going to pretend that the CIA is still on top of its game, that clandestine operations are still worth the price tag and that military contractors can rid the world of terrorists with $700 toilet seats, so be it. So be it. I'll just carry on as the insurgent, the heretic, the purported double agent. Unpatriotic, in their eyes. But I see myself in a different role. I am a defender of liberty. It's a new world (order), so I will play the role of Daniel Boone and Davy Crockett. I will be an explorer in search of truth, justice, and the American way.

This is not just my raison d'etre, it is my *raison d'état*!

As much as I want to flay the Grand Old Party, my pump-priming is a call to democracy lovers and opposition-party partiers everywhere. King George II's approval rating is in a tailspin, so hit hard, people. Now is the time. The elephant is up against the ropes—somebody just has to land the fatal blow! I know that I'm ready to come out swinging. I'm prepared to do my duty as a citizen of the greatest country on earth. Not the only country, my fellow countrymen, family, friends, wife—but certainly the one with the most egalitarian of intentions.

Like the handyman's special I was raised in, America is a home worthy of love, despite the occasional leaky pipe and the mice in the walls. It would be a mistake to move to Canada, just as it would be a mistake to pretend these problems don't exist. It's home improvement time and I'm ready to wield the hammer. There's work to be done if this house is to be a home.

In every election in American history both parties have their clichés. The party that has the clichés that ring true wins.
—Newt Gingrich

They're extreme. We're mainstream, and we're going to stand up and fight back.
—John Kerry

11

That in view of the necessity of battling for the first principles of republican government, and against the schemes of aristocracy, the most revolting and oppressive with which the earth was ever cursed, we will cooperate and be known as Republicans until the content is terminated.
—Platform of the Grand Old Party back when it was young

Chapter One

In the "Name" of the Republicans

What we have here is a fail'yuh to communicate.

Well, actually, what we have here is a republican *system* of government built on democratic *ideals*. This means that everything distasteful about our government (bureaucracy, graft, all that faux applause during the Stage of the Union address) is to be associated with the word "republican" while everything honorable and good can be associated with the word "democratic." Well, it's almost that easy.

The republicans of Rome laid the foundation for modern-day civil law. The emperors ruled of their own accord, so democracy was absent, but in studying the Roman Empire and the democratic elements of the Athenian Senate, these Ancients must be considered our forefathers, for better or for worse. Imagine them in their great halls: the breezy robes, busty women hand-feeding them grapes, bacchanalia in the name of the common man. At least the Romans built

> A liberal is a person who believes that water can be made to run uphill. A conservative is someone who believes everybody should pay for his water. I'm somewhere in between: I believe water should be free, but that water flows downhill.
> —Theodore H. White

aqueducts for their people. Our Republicans stop short at paying for a shoddy sewage system. And we all know in what direction the elephant dung flows.

Res public is Latin for "public affair" and means that the people shall rule through their representatives, the public officials. By definition, the Republicans should be interested in the well-being of each and every American. But I haven't been hand-fed grapes in years. (Okay . . . ever.) Maybe this is because I'm a dyed-in-the-flannel Independent. I wore a toga to a party once, but woke up in the buff. I'm just better off without those kinds of parties, I guess—toga *and* Republican. There just isn't time in my life for bacchanalia and I'm sure it doesn't really fit into your schedule, either.

Modern-day Republicans. Country-club Republicans. Tightwad, old-school, blue-blood, Ivy-League, red-meat, and single-malt Republicans. The GOP is the place to be, rockin' to the beat quite naturally. Gettin' jiggy wit—well, maybe not. But they certainly do walk to the beat of their own drummer. It's a duck walk of a strut I haven't quite figured out yet. And as much as I'd like to play a round at the club and although my cholesterol count belies my love of filet mignon, I just cannot imagine myself partying with that party. Even if the Republican life was my own, I wouldn't be able to live that way for long. I'd wither like dead flowers under such a sheltered existence. I can't help but be aware of life on the other side of the tracks.

Ever since Honest Abe was shot in the head by a conservative, the Republicans have turned a blind eye to the majority and even to their own roots, the foundation of the supposed Grand Old Party. They have become disengaged. There has definitely been a fail'yuh to communicate.

> To be conservative requires no brains whatsoever. Cabbages, cows, and conifers are conservatives, and are so stupid they don't even know it.
> —Colin Welch

Back in the 1800s, opponents of the Kansas-Nebraska Act got themselves organized. *Uncle Tom's Cabin* was on everyone's lips, so on July 6, 1854, Joseph Medill put together the first official meeting of the Republican Party. Or was it? Jackson, Michigan, was the site of this caucus, but a few months earlier, a similar meeting had taken place in Ripon, Wisconsin. The GOP therefore has two birthplaces. Appropriate enough, since the party was born of an abolitionist mother and a patriotic father; a man so concerned with his fellow man that in some places it was not referred to as the Republican Party but the People's Party.

This genealogy serves as a contrast. How far the mighty have fallen. How they have forsaken their father.

> No one has ever seen a Republican mass meeting that was devoid of the perception of the ludicrous.
> —Mark Twain

The new kids on the block quickly gained momentum. Their hearts were more bubbly and pure than a Drew Barrymore romantic-comedy when, in 1856, they held their first national convention, in Philadelphia. All of the northern states were represented, as was the controversial Kansas. Four slave states also sent delegates. No togas. No grapes. No bustiness. The Republicans put their heads together and came up with John C. Frémont, a hero of the Mexican War and a man who had spent significant time pioneering out West. His nickname, "The Pathfinder," had as much to do with these experiences as with progressive political ideology, and the GOP was sure that he could lead the United States down the path of righteousness. It was not to be.

Frémont got the party off on the wrong foot by losing to James Buchanan and the Democrats. An indicator of future underachievement: The Republican Party was almost snuffed out by a rival party known, self-effacingly enough, as the "Know Nothings." They drew away votes and members and, all in all, it was an inauspicious beginning for the GOP.

The indoctrination of the handfed fat cats was still a few years away. Only once Reconstruction was said and done did the togas make their stateside appearance. Only once Ulysses S. Grant took office did the Republicans figure out that they could have their bacchanalia and get reelected, too.

In the meanwhile, though, they had to wait only four years after Frémont's loss to make a splash at the national level. The Know Nothings really didn't "know nothing" and *Elephas maximus* proved that this party was built to last. Their first true hero was arguably the greatest leader the nation has ever known. He is certainly the greatest Republican president, able to bring together the Republican system and those Democratic ideals. The original Great Communicator, tall as a tree and just as straight: Abraham Lincoln.

Stand with anybody that stands right. Stand with him while he is right and part with him when he goes wrong.
—Abraham Lincoln

Intelligence gathered by this and other governments leaves no doubt that the Iraq regime continues to possess and conceal some of the most lethal weapons ever devised.
—King George II

Chapter Two

The GOP Timeline: From Honest Abe to King George II

I like to say the word *despot* out loud. French words really are a boon to the tongue. They make conversation fun; a gift to supplement our language, just as the Statue of Liberty was a gift to celebrate our democratic ideals. Over the last two years we seem to have forgotten the *raison* for this gift. Its significance.

Although not as fun to say out loud, I still ask for *French* fries. I make like Pepe LePew and hold my nose as I say *politique*. I look at the GOP's number-one chicken hawk and say, *"Despot! Despot! Despot!!!"*

George W. Bush is a new-age despot. So dictatorial is King George II that members of his own party are starting to turn on him. I have no sympathy for their *raison d'état*, as it took a hit to their wallets before they saw the light. The president has bitten off more than he can chew (pretzel, anyone?), and, as Bush attempts to juggle serious foreign and domestic issues, balls are being dropped left and right. Left and Right.

On the other end of the GOP timeline is Abraham Lincoln. Now he was a leader capable of handling the domestic and the foreign. I think the magic was in his stovepipe hat, like Bill and Ted's excellent phone booth and Dorothy's ruby-red slippers. There's no place like home, and King George II likes to dress up when he goes home to Crawford. He's got his *Urban Cowboy* belt buckle, but I don't think that's going to cut the mystical mustard.[7]

Honest Abe, born in a log cabin in Hardin, Kentucky, in 1809, was frontier, through and through. That boy was country. King George II is about as country as Shania Twain. He's all sparkle and implants.

In 1862, Honest Abe pushed the Homestead Act through, as well as the Morrill Land Grant Act. Morrill gave quite a boost to public education and was responsible for the founding of Michigan State and Pennsylvania State universities. He made sure construction of a transcontinental railroad would be funded and lent his support to a national banking system. Honest Abe was a little slow in freeing the slaves, but when he felt the time was right, humanity reigned supreme. Well, it's almost that easy.

There is a small monument in the middle of a field in Pennsylvania. It marks the spot

20

---

[7] Should I ever bump into Dubya on the streets of New Haven, I'll have to ask, "Does John Travolta know you've got his belt buckle?"

Now you'll be glad to know the president will practice safe snacks.
—Laura Bush, on
The Tonight Show

Home is a name, a word, it is a strong one;
stronger than magician ever spoke, or spirit ever
answered to, in the strongest conjuration.
—Charles Dickens

where Lincoln gave his Gettysburg Address. You can bet that someday when King George II gets his monument it will be anything but
understated. I predict something similar in size to the Washington
Monument, but in the shape of an oil derrick. The only question is
where? Texas? Iraq? Afghanistan? Alaska? Regardless, a moneymak-
ing machine that gives the shaft again and again and again will be a
fitting tribute to the boy who would be king.

Both men are indubitably linked by the name of their political party, but what's in a name? Can it possibly mean the same
thing now as it did one hundred and fifty years ago? To find the
truth, you might think we have to dig down deep, like oil-well
deep. But actually, the answer lies pretty close to the surface, as
shallow as an apology from Trent Lott. No, the name is not the
same. The Grand Old Party has changed drastically since its days as
the Grand Young Party.

King George II and Honest Abe might as well have been
Oscar and Felix; about as much in common as their two versions of
the party. Lincoln was a war
hawk only when his hand
was forced. He was a saber
rattler who really did want
the ballot to be stronger than
the bullet. Meanwhile, the
crowned prince of Kenne-
bunkport was raised to be a

21

What is conservatism? Is
it not adherence to the
old and tried, against the
new and untried?
—Abraham Lincoln

Poor George, he can't help it. He was born with a silver foot in his mouth.
—Ann Richards

war hawk all too willing to use that saber. He continues to see, despite skipping out on Vietnam, the bullet as a means of ensuring the ballot.

At opposite ends of the GOP timeline: the Odd Couple.

Lincoln took care of business during his presidency. He took responsibility for the Union Army, firing several generals until he hit the right combination and the war was won. Little Boy Bush took care of business by ruining a few—the name Harken harkens back to his years of drink, drug, and depleted value—before turning to politics. From trading away Sammy Sosa as owner of the Texas Rangers to ruining the schools and the environment as Texas's governor, it only makes sense that he would be promoted up, up, and away to president. Of course, having his brother take care of business in Florida didn't hurt . . .

By contrast, Honest Abe, whose father was a big-time Whigger (i.e., a member of the Whig Party), got out from under his father's shadow and achieved election all on his own. He started by winning a seat in the House of Representatives, then made the natural progression to the Senate. During divisive times, he somehow managed to gain the approval of the majority. And in the midst of this ascension, he was called on, time and time again, to speak out against an able opponent: conservative Democrat Stephen A. Douglas. King George II had no such verbal challenges and, given his grasp of the English language, this was a good thing for the First Family.

If you want to know what God thinks of money, just look at the people he gave it to.
—Dorothy Parker

22

> Consider the vice president, George Bush, a man so bedeviled by bladder problems that he managed, for the last eight years, to be in the men's room whenever an important illegal decision was made.
> —Barbara Ehrenreich

While Lincoln traveled the country, debating Douglas on the issue of slavery, King George II continually commandeers Air Force One for fund-raising jaunts. Ah, the parallels.

Truth be told, King George II would probably be getting away with it if times were better; if the national debt wasn't increasing faster than an Atkins-induced cholesterol count. But unless you consider veils, donkey carts, and mountain bread to be weapons of mass destruction, chances are you'll be giving your support elsewhere come Election Day. When asked about those sixteen infamous words, history came very close to repeating itself. You could just tell that King George II wanted to say that he was in the bathroom when the CIA report was reviewed. Just like Big Daddy Bush during Iran-Contra.

Flush, flush, and the elephant dung flows down.

Ironically enough, early on in the war King George II landed on an aircraft carrier just off of the coast of Schwarzifornia. That ship: the USS *Abraham Lincoln*. And get this, my fellow conspiracy theorists: Lincoln's secretary once planted a bush. And Bush's secretary drives a Lincoln!

> When he put on that flight suit, it was one more time than he ever wore it with the National Guard.
> —Allan Colmes

Big Daddy Bush may have gotten away with the commode excuse, but I doubt that the crowned prince of Kennebunkport can pull it off, flight suit or no flight suit. Whereas Honest Abe served admirably in his war, our forty-third president split time between the Texas and Alabama National Guard, all to avoid Vietnam. I don't mean to say I'm in favor of war and I certainly don't mean to say that I wouldn't have hidden behind my father's connections (had he had any other than at the lumberyard), but I do draw the line at telling others to go where I would not go and to do what I would not do. Honest Abe would agree.

The Republican Party of King George II has been a long time in the making. From Bob Packwood the adulterer to Trent Lott the segregationist to William J. Bennett the compulsive gambler to Strom Thurmond the gambling segregationist adulterer . . . If they'd only continued to follow Honest Abe's example, the GOP closet would be without most of its skeletons. Then again, the First Family wouldn't have one president to its credit, let alone two.

Standing behind the podium in that field in Pennsylvania, Lincoln was no less resigned to reuniting the Union, but his words were a little worse for the wear of war. "The world will little note nor long remember what we say here."

He was wrong about Gettysburg, just as King George II was wrong about those WMDs. So, I guess they have that in common. Still, I doubt there will ever be a Bush Bedroom in the White House, let alone a King George II monument anywhere other than in Crawford.

You can fool some of the people all of the time,
and all of the people some of the time, but you
cannot fool all of the people all of the time.
—Abraham Lincoln

All private interests, all local interests,
all banking interests, the interests of individuals,
everything, should be subordinate now to
the interest of the government.
—Senator John Sherman (R-OH),
foreshadowing King George II's philosophy

It is sometimes said that Christianity has always
had its own form of psychoanalysis in the practice
of confession
—R. S. Lee, in *Freud and Christianity*

Chapter Three

Adam in the Garden:

Monday

"Hello? Are you in there, Father Mark?"

"Yep. That's me."

"My name's Adam? I'm here for your 'Convention Confession?'"

"Fantastic. You sound young. Twenty-four?"

"Close, Father. I'm twenty-one, actually."

"Damn. I'm usually right on when playing the numbers. But hey, the good Lord works in mysterious ways. Ever-living, ever-loving, forever and ever, amen. Ever gone to confession in a sports arena before, kid?"

"No. I keep expecting to hear the National Anthem!"

"You just might, here at 'the world's most famous arena.' 'We Will Rock You' should certainly be in every hymnal. That Freddie Mercury had one queer eye for the *queer* guys."

"That's not necessarily true, is it Father?"

"Did you just fall off of the apple cart or what? That guy was more dippy than—anyway, what can I do for you, Adam?"

"I've come to confession tonight, well, because I feel like a liar being here."

"You weren't invited?"

"I was, in a way. I'm officially listed as an alternate."

"So, Apple Cart, we've got something in common."

"Okay . . . See, I'm with the delegation from Montana and well, my confession is . . ."

"Go on. Spit it out."

"Well, I'm not really a Republican. I'm an Independent."

"What?! A traitor in our midst? Security!"

"But I thought you were here to help, Father?"

"I'm just playing with you, Apple Cart. You're young and you have much to learn. Just know that everyone becomes a Republican in the end."

"You really think so?"

"Oh, sure. And don't worry about being an Independent. It actually works in my favor, you being an alternate and all."

"How so?"

The Republican convention: an event with the intellectual content of a Guns 'n' Roses lyric attended by every insurance broker in America who owns a pair of white shoes.
—P. J. O'Rourke

"Here's the deal. The Republican National Committee wants to create a strong sense of piety here, so they hired me. They hired all of us in these little booths here, sprinkled around the holy land that used to be the blue seats. Monks and rabbis, priests and ministers. I was a last-second replacement. An alternate just like you, Apple Cart. The Episcopal priest was here last night but nobody came to see him, so he said he wouldn't be back. Go figure . . ."

Thus one can observe that those who proclaim piety as their goal and purpose usually turn into hypocrites.
—Johann Wolfgang Von Goethe

"But the sign said *you* were Episcopalian. That's what my parents raised me to be. An Anglican WASP and a Republican, through and through."

"Episcopalian . . . Universalist . . . What's the difference? I live just on the other side of the Lincoln Tunnel, so I figured, what the hell? Meet some people and earn a couple of bucks, right?"

"I'm sorry. I don't understand, Father Mark."

"Tom."

"Excuse me?"

"My name is Tom. The other guy was Mark. I'm Tom. *Reverend* Tom, if that makes you feel any better."

"This has been such a confusing day. I've never been out of Montana before."

"Don't worry, Apple Cart. I'll take care of you."

"But why are *you* here, Reverend Tom?"

"I'm here because the RNC got together with Madison Square Garden and decided it'd be a good idea to offer confession every night. You know, to make sure all you boys behave. I guess Philly is still recovering from 2000!"

"Well, I'm certainly glad you all are here. I'm more used to confessing directly to God, but it's good to have someone to talk to. So, can I confess now? I need to call home before bed."

"Shoot, my little infidel."

"Well, the Republican Party is nice enough to have me here and all, so I'm just feeling kind of guilty about it."

"Ah, it's refreshing to hear somebody admit their guilt."

"Thank you, Father Tom."

"Reverend."

"Reverend."

"I'm a method actor, my little Adam bomb, so I thrive on this kind of raw emotion. I've been an ordained minister of the Universalist Church for almost ten years now, but I'm still waiting for my breakthrough role. I was able to marry two of my friends in Central Park, but no paying jobs yet unless you count this one. I'm still holding out hope, though, you know? Rabbi Goldstein, Father Sarducci, the Dalai Lama, I don't care. I'll play anyone."

"Well, I don't know much about acting, but I do know that I feel bad about being an Independent and still coming here this week. I kind of did it just so I could see New York, you know?"

"An accidental tourist. Cute. Well, don't you worry . . . The Reverend Tom will set you back on the path of righteousness. You haven't killed anyone, have you, Apple Cart?"

"Nope."

"You don't cheat on your taxes?"

"Nope."

"You've never banged your neighbor's wife?"

Thou shalt not speak ill of another Republican.
—Ronald Reagan, referring to the
Eleventh Commandment

> Where is it written in the Constitution that you may take children from their parents, and parents from their children, and compel them to fight the battles of any war in which the folly or the wickedness of government may engage it?
> —Daniel Webster

"Father!"

"Reverend."

"Reverend."

"Good. I'll take that as a no. Fixing you up shouldn't be a problem, then. Let's get to it. I need a smoke."

"Okay, *Reverend* Tom."

"Look, I'm legit, kid. I know my sacrament of reconciliation and my seal of confession and all that other business, so fear not. Praise Jesus, we'll get through this together. Now, this guilt of yours . . . What does it feel like? Is it a weight upon thy heart, like a fat lady in your lap, or is it more of a cloud across the mind, like the bittersweet smoke of an unfiltered?"

"Well, I just kind of hung out last night and got a feel for the place. And today, the action started to pick up a bit. But I still don't feel very comfortable here. There are so many reasons, but I'll give you one, for an example. I hate the idea of my vote leading to a soldier's death. Some poor guy my age, dying just to give us a foothold in the

> I will never apologize for the United States of America—I don't care what the facts are.
> —Big Daddy Bush, on the shooting down of an Iranian airliner by the U.S.

Middle East. And I certainly don't want to cast the vote that costs women the right to choo—"

"Oh, Christ . . . Not another spineless liberal."

"I haven't gone to church regularly since before college, but should you be using the Lord's name in vain like that?"

"My booth. My confessional. My rules. Now, what's your story, Adam? You're starting to sound like one of those kids who goes to school on the short bus."

"Excuse me?"

"Forget it. Look, Apple Cart, these questions of yours, they'll all be answered with your first paycheck. End of story."

"What do you mean?"

"People living at home have the time, energy, and mistaken idealism to be Democrats—or Independents. Once you start getting up every day to haul boxes or wait tables, you'll see. You won't want one dime going to crack whores."

"I hope to never be so cynical, Reverend Tom."

"Good luck, Adam. I mean it."

"You know, as a freshman I wasted a vote on Nader. After that, I spent the next two years complaining about Bush along with all the Democrats, but I never bought into the whole college-communism-Castro thing. So, as a senior I started attending Young Republican meetings and listening to talk radio. My father got so excited that he called in a favor—and here I am. I haven't told him yet that I like Colmes more than Hannity. Or that I think Imus is a closet liberal."

"Blasphemy! Imus is a warrior. A New York icon. I wet my whistle with him one night, many years ago . . . You've been reading too much of *The New York Times* and listening to too many professors—but there's nothing I can do about that right now, and I really, really need that cigarette. Come on back tomorrow if you're still feeling guilty, and we'll talk."

"Okay . . ."

"What is it, kid?"

"Well, I don't really feel any better. Any other time I've made my confession, it's just been me and the good Lord. I don't really feel like He was here in the booth tonight."

"You liberals are all alike. Speed your way through confession like it's a car wash and then get upset when you don't feel clean. It's no wonder you're all so quick to sin again. Sheesh."

"This is something only liberals are guilty of?"

"Touché. You get to leave on a high note . . . Okay, that'll be twenty dollars, please."

"But this is supposed—"

"Yeah, yeah, yeah."

"Reverend Tom, I don't think I want to pay to go to confession."

"I'll make you a deal, Apple Cart. Ten dollars per confession and I won't shortchange you. At least fifteen minutes per confession. Not a bad deal in a place where hot dogs go for three-fifty."

"I don't know . . ."

"Good. It's settled. Leave the money on the folding chair and come again."

"One last thing before I go, Reverend."

"Shoot."

"Well, when I walked to the hotel yesterday, it was still light out. I'm a . . . I'm a little nervous now. You know, because it's getting dark out."

"Come on, Apple Cart. This is confession, not kindergarten!"

"Right. Sorry. It's just I've only ever been to Helena before. You know, for school."

Liberal Doctrine: it is not children who misbehave, but parents.
—Mason Cooley, in *City Aphorisms*

33

"Just open your little piggy bank and sport for the cab. He'll get you back to the hotel, safe and sound. All right?"

"Okay."

"And no more reading *The Times*, Apple Cart. Watch Tucker Carlson, instead."

"Thanks, Reverend. Have a good night."

"You, too. Try and get some sense."

"Excuse me?"

"I said, 'Try and get some sleep.' G'night."

Dear Lord,

I made a new friend tonight. He's a real, bona fide New Yorker! Tough exterior, but a big heart. We spoke about politics, but only a little. Religion, too. The plane ride and the hotel and Madison Square Garden . . . It's all so exciting! I feel like a fish out of water, but that's all right. I've got Reverend Tom to look out for me, so I am filled with hope.

I have many questions to answer for myself and tomorrow's another big day, so I'd better get some sleep. It's hard going to bed knowing that there's an entire city out there, but I've got bigger things to deal with. It's more than who I'll vote for this year. I'd like to be true to my father, but that's becoming harder and harder. Still, I sure do appreciate being here. I know to appreciate an opportunity when it comes along!

Thank you for this opportunity, for your patience, and for sending a shepherd to guide me.

Now I lay me down to sleep . . .

At home one relies on parents;
away from home one relies on friends.
—Chinese proverb

It is the confession, not the priest,
that gives us absolution.
—Oscar Wilde

Republicans sleep in twin beds—some even in separate rooms. That is why there are more Democrats.
—Will Stanton

Chapter Four

The Elephant Finds Its Feet

Somewhere between the Fourteenth Amendment and the string of four-and-out-the-door presidents, the GOP got its nickname as well as its symbol: *Elephas maximus*. The elephant. Dumbo.

If you are an animalphile, you already know that a male elephant is a bull. A baby is a calf and a female is a cow. (Think Tammy Faye Baker.) The oldest elephant on record lived for ninety-eight years, surpassed only by Strom Thurmond. And a Snapple-cap fact: Despite having four knees, elephants are the only animal in the world that cannot jump. Good thing Dumbo had those magic cars. One of the most amazing things about the elephant is the trunk; more on that later. I've amused the animalphiles for long enough, and it's time now to get back to the politics.

One particular cartoonist gets credit for cementing the place of the elephant and the donkey in our political culture. When *The

> The elephant has a thick skin, a head full of ivory, and as everyone who has seen a circus parade knows, proceeds best by grasping the tail of its predecessor.
> —Adlai Stevenson

Herald, a New York newspaper, was editorializing against Republican president Ulysses S. Grant, Thomas Nast lampooned the paper's editors with a donkey in disguise, dressed like a lion and roaring to scare voters.

"One of the animals frightened by the donkey's roar of Caesarism," writes congressional historian, Ilona Nickels, "was an elephant—a symbol for Republican voters, who were abandoning President Grant, and in Nast's view, about to fall into the Democrats' trap."

Other cartoonists picked up on the idea and just like that, America's leading political parties had their symbols. Although the Democrats have been somewhat hesitant to embrace the jackass, and understandably so, the GOP has been more than happy to associate themselves with the elephant. They choose to see their mascot as an emblem of strength and intelligence, even while the rest of the world looks at it as a clumsy behemoth that charges through African villages once a year to maintain his due deference; an animal that rolls in its own feces to cool off; that walks trunk to tail to trunk to tail to trunk to tail so that no one gets lost.

I don't mean to imply that I hate elephants. And I certainly don't have anything against Dumbo. I think that a flying elephant is good, clean, wholesome fun. But you see, here we go again! Republicans are absolutists—all-or-nothingists—while the rest of us are apologists. I almost hate to say "apologists" because the Republicans have turned it into a cussword. I'm talking about being a human being; a problem solver who tries to look at the whole picture and not just what a situation means to the wallet. Even if Dumbo cost me a few extra bucks I would have a hard time hating him. Then again, his kind is responsible for my school having a nurse only one day a week. (We tell the kids that they can only get sick on Thursdays . . .) And it *is* Dumbo who continues to pay defense contractors even though they owe back taxes to the tune of $3 billion.[8] Dumbo, who is religiously opposed to stem cell research and the distribution of condoms and clean needles. Dumbo, who cringes at the thought of gay marriage and who thinks that the death penalty is moral, but that abortion is immoral. Really, though, there is very little room in this teacher's heart for hate. I can find the good in people and even in elephants (as long as they can fly).

While I'm feeling complimentary, I might as well point out that *Elephas maximus* falls into the same category of "primitive hoof-animals" as the lovable manatee. And, believe it or not, elephants actually have thumbs. Or at least one thumb. That's right: one opposable thumb . . . on the end of their trunks! The elephant has actually evolved faster than the governor of California.[9] Go figure.

From emblematic elephants to truncated nicknames . . . The bottom line is that GOP takes up a lot less headline space than REPUBLICANS. Knowing that, it shouldn't be surprising to learn that it was a journalist who first came up with the three-letter abbreviation for "Grand Old Party." This was right around the time Nast was sketching that scared little elephant.

---

[8] Four knees, four legs—and still, the elephant cannot jump. It's like having a multibillion-dollar Defense Department and not being able to win the war.

[9] Maria is hoping that by the time her great-grandchildren are born, Arnie's genes will have been bred out, allowing for opposable thumbs and less back hair.

The first verified use of "GOP" dates back to October 15, 1884: THE G.O.P. DOOMED read the front page of the *Boston Post*. If only headlines didn't lie. The Grand Old Party is still far from "doomed," unfortunately.

In 1875 there was a reference to "this gallant old party" in the *Congressional Record*, but according to *Harper's Weekly*, the *Cincinnati Commercial* was the first to use the "Grand Old Party" in full form. This was in the centennial year of 1876. It was only a matter of time before some editor shortened it to "GOP," saving his publication thousands of dollars and earning himself a hefty raise and a promotion. Because that's how it always works, right? I don't mean to sound cynical. I'm still too young to be a grumpy old man, but hey, there's an idea! Why not "Grumpy Old Men" for the Republicans, instead? "GOM" is perfect.

GOP has been an abbreviation for other phrases, as well; phrases that aptly represent the party of Dumbo and Dumbya. Like in the *Dukes of Hazzard*, how about good ol' boys? GOB . . . I can just see the headlines: "GOB-STOPPERS NIX FUNDING," "GOB HOBNOB AT FUND-RAISER," "NRA GETS A-OK FROM GOB." There's definitely some potential there.

The last time a new century introduced itself, automobiles were just starting to gain in popularity. Motoring through the countryside, a Republican might direct his hired help to "get out and push" after stalling. "GOP" became a colloquialism for this directive and reminds me of the GOP approach to jump-starting a stalled economy. (Hoover and Reagan just never could understand why the unemployed weren't getting out and pushing.)

In the last half of the twentieth century, the Republicans flirted with being hip, and you can guess how that went. It was during the 1964 presidential campaign that the term "Go-Party" was used briefly. Then, during the Nixon Administration, frequent references were made to the "generation of peace." Ah, Nixon in patchouli, dancing to The Grateful Dead and sending messages of peace, love, and understanding. All except for the fact that he liked to get bombed and then bomb Cambodia. It's to be expected that the GOP name would fall prey to irony from time to time. You can't blame the Republicans for trying, though. Like a kid brother claiming supremacy, the party had to figure out a way to deal with their inferiority complex. The Democratic Party was a whole generation older, and how can you call yourself "Old," let alone "Grand," when compared to an organization jump-started by Thomas Jefferson?

You can't. These are the details *Elephas maximus* has conveniently forgotten over the years, despite that supposed long memory. What else can you expect from an animal that has four knees but can't jump?

41

The Democrat represented the faith in
the responsibility of the individual.
The Republican represented a faith in
centralized power.
—Beatrice Webb, on the Republican Party
during the Gilded Age[10]

---

[10] And today, perhaps?

Public money is like holy water; everyone helps himself to it.
—Italian proverb

Chapter Five

Elephas maximus: From Useless S. Grant to Wobbly Willie

Four years after Lincoln was shot, the White House became *La Maison de Opulence.* Corrupt may not be a French word, but it sure is an appropriate way to describe the Republican Party's second president, the original fat cat, Ulysses S. Grant.

"Let no guilty man escape," Grant proclaimed, "if it can be avoided . . . No personal considerations should stand in the way of performing a duty." He was commenting on government officials implicated in the Whisky Ring (distillers who'd defrauded the government), the same officials he then defended in court.[11]

---

[11] The Gold Ring and the Indian Ring haunt his legacy, as well.

> Liberty means responsibility. That is why most men dread it.
> —George Bernard Shaw

Emerging from the Civil War with a squeaky clean image—other than getting bombed à la Nixon before battles—General Grant quickly soiled the White House with his scandals; so much so that a number of anti-Grant Republicans joined with the Democrats to nominate Horace Greeley in 1872. Greeley lost and the infighting continued throughout Grant's second term. Republicans were fond of waving "the bloody shirt," reminding their constituents of the negative feelings of the Civil War and trying to convince them that the party was still fighting the good fight. It was obvious, though, that the platform of principles had been replaced by one of greed. And Grant was at the helm of that shady ship.

In the years following the passage of the Fifteenth Amendment, universal suffrage went into effect—just as long as your definition of "universal" doesn't include women, impoverished and illiterate African-Americans, Asians, and Native Americans. Most of these equal-opportunity infractions took place in the Dirty South as part of the defiant Jim Crow laws. Despite his military background, Grant just couldn't instill order; the nation would have been better off if this Ulysses hadn't made his way home from war.[12] Intimidation of African-Americans was rampant, and as Lewis L. Gould writes of the GOP, "The earlier generation that had opposed slavery and fought the Civil War was giving way to professional politicians who approached their calling with less concern for ideology and more for their continued electoral survival."

Under Useless S. Grant, the Republican Party put its full

44

---

[12] His own father nicknamed him "Useless."

force behind the kind of economic growth that could only further perpetuate the differences between rich and poor. The Industrial Revolution was in full effect, laissez-faire was the order of the day, and soon battles of skin color and nationality would be joined by social class conflict.

A propensity for cigars eventually saw the general-turned-president buried in Grant's Tomb, and the next four elections would be narrowly won by Republican candidates, Rutherford B. Hayes among them. His victory over Samuel Tilden was so close that the Democrats actually parlayed their concession into the resumption of control in the South.[13] Reconstruction was over. The trade-off of Hayes wasn't really worth it for the GOP, nor the nation, as "His Fraudulency" was as corrupt as they come during his campaign and as virginal as a nunnery during his presidency. His four years in the Oval Office would be a church social in comparison to his predecessor's.

Hayes didn't booze it up like Grant, and in fact, he banned alcohol from the White House, precluding him from including the finest minds of the day in his cabinet. Who wants to be around a goody-two-shoes for four years? (Hayes was the first of the four-and-out-the-door

Five friends are made cold or hostile for every appointment; no new friends are made. All patronage is perilous to men of real ability or merit. It aids only those who lack other claims to public support.
—Rutherford B. Hayes, nineteenth president of the United States of America

---

[13] Hayes lost by more than 250,000 popular votes. Sound familiar?

> My God! What is there in this place that a man should ever want to get into?
> —James A. Garfield, on the presidency

GOP presidents.) So saintly was the White House that Hayes's gospel-singing, pro-prohibition wife was known as Lemonade Lucy.

Lemonade Laura and his fraudulency, King George II, had nothing on the Family Hayes.

James A. Garfield spent one year as president of the United States, outdoing all those four-and-out-the-door Republicans. Yes, it's true: the job he hated so much actually killed him.

Garfield eked his way into office in 1880, winning a plurality, but by a mere 39,000 votes. This was common for Republican victories during The Gilded Age. Between 1876 and 1892, the White House was theirs for all but four years; yet the country had some serious concerns about their GOP-affiliated representatives.[14] Just as most of the Republican presidents hailed from Ohio during this time, most couldn't get themselves reelected to save their lives. Literally.

After being elected the nation's twentieth president, Garfield annoyed party boss Roscoe Conkling by neglecting to return favors. Conkling's complaints were not the exception. The Republican rule had been reward, and most supporters felt that the nepotism of Grant would pick up again after the disappointment of Hayes. It was not to be, and one of the disgruntled decided to take matters into his own hands. Charles J. Guiteau shot the incidental president on July 2, 1881, and three months later Garfield died of complications.

But let's end this section on a happier note. President Garfield *did* have his talents. As the story goes, he could actually write in Greek

---

[14] In 1890, the GOP-controlled legislature was nicknamed the Billion-Dollar Congress for being the first in American history to spend that sum.

and Latin . . . at the same time! I guess anything's possible when you have a thumb at the end of your nose.

One hundred years before Ronald Reagan took Foggy Bottom by storm, another Republican came in like a lion and went out like a lamb. At first glance, Chester A. Arthur might seem to be a Republican cut from the Grant, fat-cat cloth.[15] But like a breath of fresh air in a room cloudy with cigar smoke, he threw the window open on patronage. Unfortunately, fumigating nepotism and corruption is like dropping twenty pounds on a pizza-and-beer diet, especially when it was favors and backroom deals that put you in the Oval Office in the first place.

Arty had doubts about his ability and integrity, but all in all, his years in office showed him to be above reproach. Much like the previous GOP presidents, he'd used the political machine to reach the highest heights, but once in office was astounded by how deep the corruption ran. His efforts to fight it were trivial, including a civil

> Assassination can no more be guarded against than can death by lightning.
> —James Garfield, right before the lightning struck

> My inspiration is a Godsend to you. It raised you from a political cypher to the president of the United States.
> —Charles J. Guiteau, in a letter to Chester A. Arthur

---

[15] Cloth is right: Arthur owned more than eighty pairs of pants.

> Since I came here I have learned that
> Chester A. Arthur is one man and the President
> of the United States is another.
> —Chester A. Arthur

service reform bill. Meanwhile, several Republicans who'd enjoyed a cushy post with the Post Office were found guilty of fraud. But, Arty'd had enough; he was destined to be yet another four-and-out-the-door Republican. He didn't seek re-nomination in 1884, claiming illness, and happy to have escaped the graft of his party. Besides, he wasn't the most motivated of fellows. According to journalists assigned to trail him, Arty's philosophy was, Why do today what you could put off till tomorrow?[16]

Next up for the Republican Party was Little Ben!

Benjamin Harrison was nothing if not resourceful. He is the president who brought ferrets into the White House, after all. Why, you might ask? To get rid of the rats, of course.

Little Ben—he stood five feet, six inches tall—looked to exterminate his children in much the same fashion, freezing them out of his will. They were ticked off when he married the niece of his re-

> Rutherford B. Hayes, James A. Garfield, Chester
> Alan Arthur, and Benjamin Harrison . . . presidents
> have fallen into an obscurity that makes them
> almost indistinguishable to modern readers.
> —Lewis L. Gould

---

[16] If King George II ruled that way . . . we'd never get to Mars!

cently deceased wife. This upset Little Ben. The nerve of them . . .

But rats come in all shapes and sizes. Looking back at Harrison's campaign, there was a puppet master of a rat to see him through. His name was James Blaine. Such a rock star was Blaine that he even had fol-

> He was as glacial as a Siberian stripped of its furs.
> —Senator Thomas Platt (R-NY), on Benjamin Harrison

lowers, dubbed "Blainiacs" and "Half Breeds." It was Blaine who introduced Harrison to businessman John Wanamaker. Harrison was pro-tariff and Wanamaker wanamake him the president, so he raised money from several big corporations and just like that, America was officially introduced to campaign finance. Of course, the GOP was the first to facilitate an election bought. The process was called "frying the fat," and the elephant would be getting fat, all right. Gone were the days of fighting for civil rights, especially the rights of the poor, disenfranchised ex-slaves. After all, could the poor buy the president a home in Cape May?[17]

> Harrison will never know how close a number of men were compelled to approach the penitentiary to make him President!
> —Matt Quay, Republican Party boss from Pennsylvania

And so it was that one hundred years after George Washington was sworn in that Little Ben assumed office. He was also known as "Kid Gloves," compliments of Democrats who were making reference to Harrison's silver spoon. His great-grandfather had signed the Declaration of

---

[17] This was how Wanamaker made his overtures to Harrison.

> We were told in the old times that the rich were getting richer and the poor poorer; and to cure that imaginary ill, our political opponents have brought on a time when everybody is getting poorer.
> —Little Ben

Independence and his grandfather, William Henry Harrison, was a war hero and the ninth president of the United States.

Little Ben was no hero. His finest kill, as a matter of fact, was a farmer's pig. He apologized, explaining to the farmer that he'd thought it was a raccoon. I can live with a dead pig—nothing turns a house into a home like the smell of bacon!—what concerns me, though, is having a president who considers raccoon to be big game.

Little Ben was followed by William "Little Bill" McKinley (also known as Wobbly Willie): the Napoleon Complex had found a home. The Republican Party transformed itself from the People's Party to the Grand Old Party during this mini-run of presidential

> There never has been a time in our history when work was so abundant or when wages were as high, whether measured by the currency in which they are paid or by their power to supply the necessaries and comforts of life.
> —Little Ben, one year before the nation's worst economic depression

dominance, and it was a time when short guys ruled the roost.[18] Only Garfield was listed at six-foot and even that was a stretch.

The four-and-out-the-door trend continued with Wobbly Willie; his greatest achievement would be sitting in office when the 1900s got underway. There wasn't much centennial celebrating in the Dirty South,

> Territory sometimes comes to us when we go to war in a holy cause, and whenever it does the banner of liberty will float over it and bring, I trust, blessings and benefits to all people.
> —William McKinley

though, as segregation was being enforced with continued violence. McKinley was too concerned with retaining the white Southern vote to do much about it. Still, the few black men who could survive the trip to the polling place voted Republican, as the GOP still seemed the lesser of two evils. Because they were such a small percentage of his constituency, McKinley knew he could get away with ignoring the African-American agenda. Instead, he focused on laissez-faire policies; big business was allowed to get bigger and "trusts" were the order of the day as merger after merger was approved. In 1899 alone, more than 1,200 companies were bought. McKinley showed himself to be as lazy as he was laissez-faire.

Wanamaker had handed Harrison the keys to the Oval Office, and Ohio businessman Marcus A. Hanna was the puppet master rat of McKinley's campaign. Any good home has a cat to chase those rats away, but the Republican fat cats weren't doing a very good job.

---

[18] "McKinley was a short man at five feet six," Lewis L. Gould writes, "and he dressed to make himself seem taller than he was."

> The mission of the
> United States is one
> of benevolent
> assimilation.[19]
> —Wobbly Willie

Hanna saw the potential in Wobbly Willie's position on tariffs and the gold standard and he knew that victory spelled continued prosperity for his fellow buckeye industrialists. With the money machine behind him, McKinley set a record with $3 million in campaign funds.[20]

The Republicans held sway over all three branches of government and the nation was free to go merger-crazy.

Hanna couldn't stop a bullet, though, and McKinley was assassinated in Buffalo in 1901. He died begging for his men to go easy on the shooter, anarchist Leon Czolgosz. This lent credence to Teddy Roosevelt's insinuation that Wobbly Willie had no more backbone than a chocolate éclair. And Teddy knew backbone . . .

52

> I don't understand why someone would spend
> $2 million to get elected to a $125,000-a-year job,
> but they do it all the time.
> —Joseph Napolitano

---

[19] Now there's an oxymoron! "Benevolent assimilation" under McKinley included aiding rebels in Cuba, invading the Philippines, annexing Hawaii, and supporting the Open Door policy in China.

[20] By comparison, William Jennings Bryan, his opponent, didn't even have $100,000 to spend.

He had a way of handling men so that they
thought his ideas were their own.
—Elihu Root, on the consummate politician,
William McKinley

Time to face reality. Your elected officials have been rolling and smoking your hard-earned cash, folks. I, for one, say "Screw this!" Where are our fireworks, our donkey shows?
—Andrij Witiuk, *Maxim* candidate campaigning in 2000

Chapter Six

Adam in the Garden:
Tuesday

"Hello? Reverend?"

"Well, if it isn't Apple Cart. How's tricks?"

"Excuse me?"

"An old *Forty-second Street* question . . . Never mind. So, did you get back to the hotel all right, last night?"

"Yeah, except the cab driver got mad at me. He said my fare wasn't worth the gas out of his ass. Oops! Sorry, Reverend Tom."

"Oh, my virgin ears. Why was he so angry?"

"I'm only staying three blocks away."

"Of course you are. Now, let me assume my role because I know you've got some confessing to do . . . Do you feel *alienated* from *God*, Apple Cart?"

> It was like Groundhog Day. He popped out of a hole, and we got four more years of Bush.
> —Bill Maher, on Saddam Hussein's capture

"Uh, I guess. There are some things I'm not so sure of. Plus, I figure I'll have a family someday, so I ought to get back in touch with Him."

"That's my boy! You bring the ten bucks?"

"Yeah. Sure."

"Very good. Let's keep going then. Who have you wronged recently, my little infidel?"

"Well, I certainly haven't *wronged* President Bush. I just don't think that I want him as my president anymore. Mainly because of the war. I was upset with him before and now that he's failed to find any evidence of a 'gathering thr—'"

"Whoa! What'd I tell you about reading *The Times*, Apple Cart? Don't you want to be patriotic? A good Christian soldier?!"

"Well, sure. But, like, I keep thinking about how the Garden of Eden was basically in Iraq and how we're bombing that very same area now and killing all these innocent people there."

"Don't talk to me about geography, Adam. Talk to me about Saddam being out of power and Quadaffy Duck turning over all of his nuclear technology. Things are better because we're there. I'm serious about this stuff. I lost friends in Nam—I wasn't there myself, but that's neither here nor there—and now your generation needs to do its time. Freedom comes at a cost."

"Wow. It's a good thing I came to confess, I guess."

"Damn right!"

"Our confessional is starting to sound like the penalty box at a Rangers game."

"Well, you'd better get used to the yelling and the opinions. The Garden'll be full of 'em this week."

"This is so different from Montana."

"Just remember, these are the days of the compassionate conservative, Apple Cart. You can be a good dude and still vote Republican."

"I suppose. How did you come to know so much, Reverend Tom?"

"School of hard knocks, kid. So, how're we going to straighten you out?"

"I don't know. Right now I'm looking at fifteen years of student loans. I have a credit card with almost a thousand dollars of debt on it, and I hate that. I totally disagree with carrying any debt whatsoever. Too many Americans are digging holes for themselves and too many people think it's all right because our government is doing it, too. Mortgaging the future. The good times are really going to end quickly and harshly for a lot of people."

"President Bush is no fool. His school of hard knocks wasn't quite the same as mine, but he's been through the ringer. Nobody's tougher than a recovering addict . . . We know bullshit when we step in it, and we aren't afraid to shake it off. Bush is the best chance we've got at a sane and stable nation. Debt, shmet, I say! Business makes the world go round, and your liberal candidates don't know laissez from fair, Apple Cart. They just know lazy."

"I don't know about that . . ."

The Bush team's real vulnerability is its B.M.D.—Budgets of Mass Destruction. —Thomas Friedman

57

This is the state of the union for Wall Street, not Main Street. —Ted Kennedy, on Bush's 2004 State of the Union address

"Hey, would I lie to you?"

"No, I suppose not, Reverend Tom. But the swearing . . . This *is* the House of the Lord."

"This is Madison Square Garden, Adam. Get over yourself! Now, how was the convention today?"

"It was pretty good. I need to ask you a favor, though, before we really get into this."

"Shoot."

"Well, since I'm confessing to a person and not directly to God, I think I might feel more comfortable if I knew one or two things about *you*. So, how did you come to this place?"

"The PATH train. It's really—"

"Reverend, please. You know what I mean. Like being a reverend and a devout Republican and all. How did it happen?"

"Well, I wasn't always so holy, Apple Cart. I had my fun when I was younger. Wild, wild times . . . But those times are over now. I saw the wrongfulness of my ways. Luckily, I got my life together when I did. Otherwise, I doubt I'd be alive today."

"Did somebody help you out? Point you in the right direction?"

"Did it myself, Apple Cart. I made my own opportunities and I made the most of them. The opportunity I'm most proud of, of course, is becoming a minister. I—"

"How about before that? Like when you were my age?"

"Ohhhh, you want the dirt."

"Look at it this way—I'll be learning from your experiences. I won't have to make the mistakes that you made!"

"Nice sell job, AC. This hardly qualifies as confession, but okay. Okay. I've always been an actor and part of the glory of being an actor is having second jobs and bad habits. I've waited tables, tended bar, bounced at The FoXXXy Lady, and worked as a stage-hand, a dogcatcher, an espresso maestro, and a furniture mover. You name it, I've done it."

Name me, if you can, a better feeling than the one you get when you're half a bottle of Chivas in the bag with a gram of coke up your nose and a teenage lovely pulling off her tube top in the next seat over while you're doing a hundred miles an hour down a suburban side street.
—P. J. O'Rourke, in *Republican Party Reptile*

"Nothing to be ashamed of. But what's the FoXXXy Lady?"

"I'll explain later. First, if you must know, I did get myself into a little trouble one summer when I was around your age. I was a roadie for Blue Oyster Cult and The Moody Blues and I dabbled a bit in the drugs. Too much toot. Too, too much too too toot."

"Toot?"

"Coke, kid. Cocaine. Forget being a Knight in White Satin, I was a Knight *on* White Satin!"

"You almost seem proud."

"I'm proud to be alive and living a more meaningful life now, sure."

"'Just say no?'"

"You could say that. Another juicy mistake you'll love is that I kissed Stanley Tucci in a play once. It was this off-Broadway production. You know how those things usually go."

"No, not really, but . . ."

"I had to act my way out of my gambling troubles."

"Gambling troubles?"

"Yeah. I got myself into some debt playing backroom bingo with a couple of goombahs in Little It'ly. No big deal. I still have all my fingers and toes. Just a situation I'd rather not find myself in again."

"You've lived some life."

"I mention forging my big brother's high school diploma?"

"No."

"The fact that I'm still considered AWOL from the marines?"

"Nope."

"My stint at Rykers?"

"Rykers?"

"Jail."

"Jail?"

"Jail."

"What for?"

"A misunderstanding with a guy whose car I temporarily borrowed. How about my first wife? The one who left me because of the gambling?"

"First wife?"

"Or the second? She left because I was still married to the first."

"Two wives?"

"There was a third, too."

"Three?! Are you a Mormon?"

"Three—count 'em, three. I've got a lot of love to give, Apple Cart."

"How could you say your vows three different times to three different women?"

"It's like trying to quit smoking. Piece of cake . . . I've done it hundreds of times! But seriously, I see now that love should be sacred. The love between a *man* and a *woman*. The love between a mother and her child, unborn included. Especially unborn."

"You have any kids?"

"Fortunately, no. The marriages were all pretty quick. My

> Robert Bork's America is a land in which women would be forced into back-alley abortions, blacks would sit at segregated lunch counters, and rogue police could break down citizens' doors in midnight raids.
> —Ted Kennedy, during the nomination hearings[21]

third wife did get pregnant, but she had an abortion because we were breaking up. Pretty soon after that I became a man of the cloth."

"Why were you guys getting divorced?"

"A number of reasons, but it didn't help much that I ran her mother over."

"What?"

"Her mother was getting the paper. It was like, six in the morning, and I'd had quite an evening at Elaine's. Anyway, she was bending over, picking up *The Times*, and I ran her over. More like bumped into her. Luckily I was only driving like, five miles an hour."

"Was she all right?"

"A couple of scrapes and a dislocated shoulder. Her other arm was good enough to pound me with the paper, though. *Sunday Times*, too. Maybe that's what finally knocked some sense into me!"

"Wow . . ."

"I dropped her off at the hospital with my wife and took a little drive to look at the city as the sun was coming up. Parked on top of the Palisades. That's pretty much when I found God."

[21] Ever since Bork was denied, "Borked" has been when a nominee is voted down by political opponents, especially in the case of judges.

"Good thing you did. Someone might have been seriously injured."

"I started by being a Guardian Angel—this was all in the 1980s so it's probably a bit before your time—but anyway, shortly after, I became a serious Republican. A Reagan Republican, if you will."

"So, Republican then minister?"

"Yep. Thanks for dredging up the past, Apple Cart. Really. I feel *much* better now. I'll leave *you* the ten dollars when I go. So, learn anything worthwhile?"

"Not to sound uppity, but I doubt I'd be involved in any of that business, Reverend."

"No reason to be reborn then, I guess. Unless we call you a reborn Republican! You know, Adam, if I can do it, so can you."

"A G-o-d member of the GOP? We'll see about that. For now, I'd just like to do my confessing."

"Does it always have to be about you, Apple Cart?"

"No. I'd love to hear more about your life as one of the Sopranos."

"Fine. Back to you, Adam."

"Well, there's the Republican thing. Like, for example, I know we're in the Garden, but I hate when athletes pray for victory. Far worse, though, is when wars are fought in the name of the Lord. How can that possibly be right?"

"And the Lord said unto Apple Cart, get used to it, kid. You aren't about to undo thousands of years of history and human nature with four years of the U of M."

> He's like that guy from *Dr. Strangelove,* riding the missile screaming his guts out. He's like a crazy man.
> —Imus, on Defense Secretary Donald Rumsfeld

"I guess you're right, Reverend Tom. You know, I told my parents about you when I called home."

"Oh yeah, what'd they say? Give him the twenty dollars and quit bein' such a rube?"

"No, my father actually warned me to—"

"So, why *didn't* your father come out? I thought he was big in the GOP?"

"He is, but he's been on jury duty for like two months. It's this big case in—well, anyway, he's a decent man and he wants me to be decent, too. He wants me to be a Republican and while I'm out here he wants me to meet a lot of people and to make a lot of contacts. He's even given me a list of people to track down and say hi to. He thinks this is a good networking opportunity."

"If it were that easy, Adam, I'd be on *The Apprentice* instead of talking to you!"

"I don't get it."

"Forget it. Listen, business is like everything else in the world. It's not what you know, it's who you know."

"Yeah. He's told me that a thousand times."

"Well then, get out there and network. Find some folks to drink a beer with tonight. Make some small talk, you know? You're a nice enough guy. Break that piggy bank open again! Just beware the gay bars. Take a wrong turn in this city and next thing you know you're wearing mascara and a tiara."

> Marriage is the highest state of friendship: If happy, it lessens our cares by dividing them, at the same time that it doubles our pleasures by mutual participation.
> —Samuel Richardson

63

> Problems that face our society are oftentimes problems that, you know, require something greater than just a government program or a government counselor to solve. Intractable problems, problems that seem impossible to solve, can be solved. There is the miracle of salvation that is real, that is tangible, that is available for all to see.
> —King George II, campaigning at an AME church

"I told you, gay guys don't really bother me. It's fine with me if they want to get married. Be priests, too."

"What?! Your time's up, but this is an emergency, Apple Cart. We're going into overtime because you *do* need some straightening out. Marriage is between a man and a woman, just like the priesthood is between a man and God. Homos don't qualify for either."

"How can you speak about human beings that way?"

"I'm just talking politics here, Apple Cart."

"But you're talking religion, too. You're talking about real people."

"Politics and religion have always been one and the same. You oughta know that, college boy."

"I know it, but I don't like it. I mean, it's a new millennium. Isn't it about time we change our thinking? Like having the Ten Commandments in that courthouse in Alabama. There isn't a thing wrong with the Commandments, but the Constitution plainly states that they don't belong in a public building. I think too many Republicans confuse the Commandments with the Bill of Rights."

"Boy, somebody got the motor mouth going once I said 'Time's up.' Let's continue this tomorrow. You go back to your room, call Mom and Dad, pray a little, and then go out and get that soul of yours a loofah."

"I'll try, Reverend. There *is* Mars 2001 and the Hard Rock Café."

"Just be sure to see some things other than the tourist traps. Eat some real food, visit some cathedrals, the whole nine yards. Figure out what and who God intended you to like."

"Reverend, are you saying you think I'm a homose––"

"Don't worry about what I think, Apple Cart. Let's get you straightened out on what *you* think. And now I need that cigarette, so get lost. Just before you go, leave the ten spot on your chair, okay?"

"So, you'll be here tomorrow night?"

"Yes, my little infidel. I might even have some new stories for you. Bill Bennett and I are going to hang out tonight. He's pretty well connected, so wish me luck."

"Good luck."

Dear Lord,

I've had a bit too much to drink, but boy do I feel good! My head is ringing with the loudest, coolest music I've ever heard and I can still taste the baba ghanoush. That's right, this Montana boy ate Middle Eastern food tonight! Baba ghanoush, stuffed grape leaves, falafel, kebabs . . . And the best part is, I even went out dancing!!! It was amazing. So much fun! And finally, fiiiinally, all of these ideas in my head are starting to make sense. I mean, for the first time I feel like I'm really learning some things about myself. Like, who knew I would like hip hop? Who knew I could get a bartender's attention?

Afterwards, a bunch of us went out to eat. Not to a diner, but to this little storefront shop in the East Village. We were surrounded by tattoo parlors and people of all colors and nobody cared. We ate on the sidewalk, just talking the whole time. It was two in the morning and people were out walking their dogs! I kept asking everyone about that music, too. One guy told me about The Roots and The Black Eyed Peas and how even though they're hip hop, they play their own instruments. And this other guy told me about Atlanta and the 'Dirty South' style of rap, which I guess is different from East Coast rap, which is different from West Coast rap . . . Outkast is a Dirty South group, I guess, and I like them. Who hasn't felt like an outcast? I'm telling you, I got more out of this one night than in four years of college!

My dad's either going to be real happy or he won't be. I must admit, talking about it makes me feel a little angry. I felt angry a couple of times today. A lot of these Republicans really rub me the wrong way with all their money and the way they like to use religion as a weapon. They walk around like God's gift . . .

Forgive me, Father. I'd better shut up now. My gosh, I can see the sunrise!

I don't know about sleep, Lord. I've got so much energy right now. I've got politics and religion and hip hop from 'Hotlanta,' all of it filling me up with life, life, life. We had a cab driver from Armenia, for Christ's sa—I'm sorry. I keep forgetting myself. It's the city coursing through my veins. I want to have it all, Lord. The city and my faith. I think I can do it; have my cake and eat it, too.

All righty, then. I need to pipe down before I run out of feet to put in my mouth.

Now I lay me down to sleep . . .

Responsibility is what awaits outside
the Eden of Creativity.
—Nadine Gordimer

We ain't the problems, we ain't the villains.
It's the suckers deprivin' the truth from our
children. Freedom of speech? Yeah boy, just
watch what you say . . .
—Ice T, representing the West Coast

The Republicans have a new health-care proposal:
Just say NO to illness!
—Mark Russell

Chapter Seven

Dirty South

History has a lot to teach; so many secrets just beneath the surface of the not-so-distant past. Who would have known, for instance, that Strom Thurmond was raised a Democrat?[22] In a world where Arnold Schwarzenegger is called governor, where Rush Limbaugh is still being paid to comment on crime, nothing should be shocking.

And speaking of history, just as John Steinbeck predicted, his beloved Tom Joad is *still* among us. Not as a politician staging photo ops with an octogenarian hoping for more Metamucil, Medicaid, and *Matlock* reruns, and not as an activist leading the protests against higher greens fees and luxury taxes ("Hell no, my Jag won't go!"). No, Tom Joad continues to serve as an inspiration to the

---

[22] Or that he had an illegitimate daughter with his parents' African-American housekeeper?

masses of working classes. He was even further immortalized in 1995 by none other than "The Boss," Bruce Springsteen. A few years later, the brilliant Los Angeles band, Rage Against the Machine, remade Springsteen's "The Ghost of Tom Joad"[23] and the legend grew.

Just as literature can breathe life into these metaphorical martyrs, so too can music. Not just rock 'n' roll à la Springsteen and RATM, either. In recent years, hip hop has shown itself to be the voice of the people. It is the millennial blues.

Reality television pales in comparison to rap music in terms of providing a clear view of life in America. The sexual innuendo serves a purpose; the cussing serves a purpose; even the braggarts serve a purpose, verbalizing the hopes and dreams of millions of underprivileged kids. These are people not to be ignored. This is a genre not to be ignored.

The pulse of music by the people and for the people can still be found where it was first heard in the subtle shifts of an A, D, E blues progression: the down-home Dirty South.

Just like America, hip hop's history tells of a variety of players in a variety of places. First on the East Coast and then on the West Coast, the source of sounds has now migrated to the Third Coast: the ATL: "Hotlanta." Bling blings flashin', after-hours clubs happenin', Timberland toes tappin', and still . . . the flag controversy flap, flap, flappin' and David Duke's lips yap, yap, yappin'.

> I gotta go out and kick around and see what's wrong and see if there's something I can do about it. And you'll see me, Mama . . .
> You'll see me.
> —John Steinbeck's hero, Tom Joad

---

[23] His album of the same name is the most powerful piece of music made in the last twenty-five years. Rage Against the Machine's version is the loudest.

In Duke's online store you will find heartwarming books like *Jewish Supremacism* and *The Talmud Unmasked*, groundbreaking videos like 1915's *The Birth of a Nation* ("this classic silent black-and-white movie about the Ku Klux Klan is simply a jewel to see," raves one racist reviewer), a wide array of clothing, including the classic white wife beater for men and the super-tight tee for women, and, for the poor white supremacist, cheap as Mississippi mud, there are pins, bumper stickers, and even a "huggie" to keep your beer cold. You can also help Duke to raise money by purchasing a handsome, mesh-backed hat. Incidentally, these 1970s throw-back hats are now popular with the hip hop crowd, so get yours before they're yanked off the Web site.

> I do not mean that white people and black people should be forced to associate together in accepting their equal rights at the hands of the nation.
> —Warren G. Harding

Even all the way up here in Connecticut, Duke is trying to spread his right-wing racism. His minions like to litter cobblestone driveways with flyers while, behind the clapboards, blue-blood children search MTV, VH1, and BET for the latest from Outkast, Cee-Lo, Mystikal, David Banner, Ludacris, Bubba Sparxx, and the Nappy Roots. Republicans may control the House, but Dirty South "crunk-style" rappers control Da House. If only rappers could convince more of these kids to go out and vote when they turn eighteen . . .[24]

In 1994, "Southernplayerlisticadillacmuzik" was released, putting Outkast and the Dirty South style of rap—hardcore but not gangsta, sensitive but full of braggadocio—on the map. Ten years later,

71

---

[24] Learn about upcoming elections and even register to vote at http://www.rockthevote.org/.

> Ah ha, hush that fuss.
> Everybody move to
> the back of the bus.
> —Outkast, in
> *Rosa Parks*

they are huge, as is their home base of Atlanta. Memphis and New Orleans are other hotbeds as hungry young rappers continue to emerge. You know that the Dirty South is big when white supremacists start protesting the shows.[25]

Rare is the time that the Republican Party has been able to consider the South a stronghold. In the mid-nineteenth century, a pro-industry, anti-slavery platform made the GOP a decidedly Northern party, and for close to fifty years it stayed this way. At the turn of the century, though, the steel ripples of the Industrial Revolution had reached both coasts and the Republicans figured out that the most important constituents are those who pay in cash. Interestingly enough, their fists got tighter around their wallets even as their pockets got deeper and, just like that, Dumbo began to champion conservative economic policies.

On the timeline of American history, it is William Jennings Bryan's "Cross of Gold" speech that really marks the beginning of the liberal shift for the Democrats. Soon thereafter, rappers of the day—blues musicians like Bessie Smith and Robert Johnson, Muddy Waters and John Lee Hooker—began to ply their trade, telling the tale of everyman and setting it to music.

In 1902, as William McKinley coasted on lame-duck wings, the devil went down to Georgia (South Carolina, actually) and begat a son named James Strom Thurmond. These days, Strom rolls over in his grave every time another Dirty South rapper hears his wallet go ching-ching. After all, back when Strom was young and virile, Negroes *knew* their place. They *kept* to themselves. They did their Negro thing

---

[25] The "Chicken and Beer" show, featuring Ludacris, Chingy, and David Banner, in Casper, Wyoming, for example.

without *bothering* the superior race. Working hard for *his people*, Governor Thurmond kept South Carolina's lunch counters and water fountains divided along the color lines, just like the public schools.

But hypocrisy reigns supreme with the white supremacists, and somewhere between birth and politics, Thurmond found time to get jiggy. Apparently, he had a taste for brown sugar. Still, one is hard-pressed to joke, given Thurmond's continued insistence on racist politics. Despite the fact that he'd had a daughter with one of *them* . . .

For example, he once stood up for more than twenty-four hours straight, speaking out against desegregation. I can't imagine the man, from the looks of him in the last years of his life, wrinkly as an elephant's hide and as wobbly as Willie, standing up at all, let alone for twenty-four hours and eighteen minutes. You must really hate black people to stay on your feet for that long.[26] In speaking out against the Civil Rights Act, an act he referred to as "race mixing," Strom made filibustering an art. Neglectful fatherhood, as well.

This genre created by African-Americans is one of the few new art forms of modern times. Developed at the turn of the century, ex-slaves sang work songs filled with irony, imagery, and love—relief from the tensions of their lives. Many blues singers were recorded by talent scouts as they sang in the fields. While the blues is played all over the country today, it was of Southern origin.
—Peggy Whitley

[26] Truth is, he sat behind a desk most of the time. Was anything what it seemed with this guy?

> All the laws of Washington and all the bayonets of the army cannot force the Negro into our homes, our schools, our churches.
> —Strom Thurmond,
> representing the crusty ol' tighty whities

"The white people of the South are the greatest minority in this nation," he said in 1956. "They deserve consideration and understanding instead of the persecution of twisted propaganda."

Before clocking in as a U.S. senator for the first time, Strom had to win an election. And win he did. As a write-in candidate, he defeated Edgar Brown and received the South Carolina Democratic Party's nomination. In doing so, he became, according to Thomas Rourke of Clemson University, "The first person in U.S. history to be elected to a major office by write-in ballot." That's a lot of hate mail (maybe this is where Duke got the idea for his flyers). Strom had a different idea of what constituted a Great Society, so in 1964 he switched to the Republican Party to help Barry Goldwater lose to Lyndon B. Johnson. Four years later, Thurmond was instrumental in

> The structure of the federal system, with its fifty separate state units, has long permitted this nation to nourish local differences, even local cultures.
> —Barry Goldwater, using federalism to defend racism[27]

---

[27] The quote was in reference to his voting down the 1964 civil rights bill. He also said, "The problems of discrimination cannot be cured by laws alone." Yeah, but they sure are a nice place to start.

shoehorning Richard Nixon's jowly cheeks into the White House. Had hip hop been around in the late '60s, there would have been many a Tricky Dick reference, no doubt.

When the Democrats turned soft, embracing desegregation and rabble-rousers like Jackie Robinson, the Kennedys, and Martin Luther King Jr., Strom went GOP. It's nice to know there's a place for old racists to go—kind of like a convalescent home for the myopic. If music's view of the nation is crystal clear, Strom's was blurred by hatred and hypocrisy. I don't buy his sudden, late-in-life color blindness, either. If the man really did change, then why not recognize his daughter? Instead, he continued to pay her off.

The shameful treatment of Essie Mae Washington-Williams by good ol' boy Strom is one of those facts—hidden just beneath the surface for too, too many years—that makes it easy to hate the Republicans. The following quote is another: "I went to a church meeting the other day and all these people came up to me and you could tell they didn't know what to say. For the first time in my life, I felt shame."[28] Mary T. Thompkins Freeman, Thurmond's niece, said this shortly after the news broke of the newest family member—

> I want to say this about my state. When Strom Thurmond ran for president, we voted for him. We're proud of it. And if the rest of the country had followed our lead, we wouldn't have had all these *problems* over all these years, either.
> —Trent Lott

---

[28] The "first time"? Strom Thurmond is your uncle and this was the "first time"?!?

Williams goes to church and was a schoolteacher, yet Freeman felt shame . . . That's more than dirty. That's Dumbo, yo.

Thurmond and Trent Lott embody the Republican South. Capitalizing on fiscal frugality and the Bible, the GOP is making the land down under the Mason-Dixon Line one of its bases of operations; the launching pad of many a redistricting effort; a place where the Confederate flag can be flown without an ounce of shame. But the dirtier the Dirty South is, the louder the music will be, the longer Tom Joad will live.

I wish I could ignore racism,
but it won't let me.
—Nas, representing the East Coast

There can be no fifty-fifty Americanism in this country. There is room here for only 100 percent Americanism, only for those who are Americans and nothing else.
—Theodore Roosevelt

Chapter Eight

Elephas maximus: From Teddy Bear to Pink

Most people don't know that, as a boy, Teddy Roosevelt was as sickly and feeble as the other President Roosevelt. Whereas FDR's experiences made him empathetic, Teddy Bear's turned him into a macho macho man. His disdain would quickly manifest itself in an "If I can do it, so can you!" mentality.

The problem with such clichés is that the details are allowed to conveniently fall by the wayside. Like, for example, the fact that as a boy, Teddy Bear's parents could afford to hire private tutors so that he didn't miss out on any schooling. Or the fact that once he found himself physically able, his family turned part of their *mansion* into his own *personal gym*. If only a hotel could be transformed into a nunnery, Paris Hilton's image might likewise be remade . . .

> The pacifist is as surely a
> traitor to his country and
> to humanity as is the
> most brutal wrongdoer.
> —Theodore Roosevelt,
> going the mucho
> macho route

Teddy went on to be a boxing star at Harvard, while FDR never freed himself from that wheelchair—and this might have ultimately forged the distinction between the two. Thinking in those terms, I say score one for infirmity: FDR was wise with his experiences while it took Teddy Bear years to move beyond his stunted adolescence.

But all was not lost. Teddy Bear did eventually grow up, learning the difference between right and wrong. He fought to have "In God We Trust" removed from American currency and was even awarded the Nobel Peace Prize in 1906. Almost as impressive was his defection from the GOP in 1912. The Republican Party had fallen under the control of ultraconservatives, so Teddy Bear joined up with the Progressives. At this point, he was liberal enough to make even the future Roosevelt proud. He'd fought big business by reinstituting the Sherman Anti-Trust Act and had helped establish the Food and Drug Administration, which greatly improved the quality of life in poor, urban areas. All of you calorie counters have Teddy Bear to thank (even though he did die of arteriosclerosis) and the icing on the carb-free cake was the work he did on behalf of land conservation. No president has shown so much love for Mother Nature. By saving a bear cub, he even gave birth to America's favorite toy, the Teddy Bear.

"Standing at six-two and weeeeighing in at over three hundred and twenty-five pounds, ladies and gentlemen, the president of the United States of Aaaaamerica, William 'Big Bill' Taaaaaft!!!"

The days of Little Ben and Little Bill were definitely over and the days of the fat-cat Republican were well underway. Fat, fat, fat . . .

You have shown that you were accused of seduction and you have conclusively proved that you were guilty of rape.
—Elihu Root, after Theodore Rex incited revolution in Panama

If you are too timid or too fastidious or too careless to do your part in this work, then you forfeit your right to be considered one of the governing and you become one of the governed instead—one of the driven cattle of the political arena.
—Theodore Roosevelt

I think I might as well give up being a candidate. There are so many people in the country who don't like me.
—William Howard Taft, feeling a tad bit sorry for himself

Tafty wasn't very crafty. After riding Teddy Bear's coattails into office, he managed to anger everyone in the party with his "dollar diplomacy." He really took the Monroe Doctrine to an extreme, and this made it very easy for Woodrow Wilson and the Democrats to return to the White House. The fact that Taft, as a Republican, and Teddy Bear, as a Progressive, split the Republican vote didn't help their party's cause much, either. The GOP would be in disarray by the

> Politics makes me sick.
> —William Howard Taft,
> entering self-loathing
> territory

time Taft's four years—yes, yet another four-and-out-the-door Republican—came to an end.

Taft just didn't know how to play the game. At times, he tried to make everybody happy; other times, only himself. He even said, "I am not so constituted that I can run with the hare and hunt with the hounds." At 325 pounds, I don't think he was running with anybody! The guy couldn't even tie his own shoes. Fat, fat, fat . . .

He sure could play golf, though. Tafty was the first in a long line of Republican presidents to choose the links over overseeing his duties. Aide Archie Butt—I promise you, this name is not a fabrication—was often left to explain the president's absence. Butt was also in charge of waking the big man up. Tafty was fond of napping and would do so in cabinet meetings and even in public. Now that's what I call bringing dignity to the office.

Warren G is an old school rapper in the LBC West Coast–style, but Warren G. Harding was an old-school Republican in the O-Hi-O Yo! style. Warren G is known for rapping about bustin' a move with the ladies. Warren G. Harding, aka G Hard, aka Wobbly Warren (an obvious nod to his homeboy, Wobbly Willie McKinley), is remembered for actually doing it. With his mistress. In White House closets! Throughout his presidency, G Hard carried on this affair with a woman,

> During a visit to the czar of Russia, Taft's pants split up the seam while he was getting out of his carriage; he had to back his way out of the czar's presence to avoid exposing his backside.
> —Cormac O'Brien

What's the use of being president if you can't have
a train with a diner car on it?
—Big Bill Taft

How's the horse?
—Elihu Root, upon hearing of Taft's horseback
ride in the Philippines

It's a good thing you wasn't born a girl.
Because you'd be in the family way all the time.
You can't say "no."
—Warren G. Harding's father

Handshaking is the most pleasant thing I can do.
—G Hard

Nan Britton, who was more than thirty years his junior.[29] G Hard had
other vices, as well. He drank whiskey in the time of Prohibition and
was a prolific gambler. Just like Snoop Dogg and his Dogg Pound,
Harding had his "poker cabinet," those aides he liked to burn the
midnight oil with. He loved cards and, just like his Republican predecessor, he loved golf. And let's not forget, in true pimp style, that
both Warren G's shared an affinity for gentlemen's clubs. G Hard's favorite hangout was DC's Gayety Burlesque. Dirty, yo.

[29] Harding's wife never saw them and Harding never saw his illegitimate daughter. How presidential . . .

I don't know what to do or where to turn in this taxation matter. Somewhere there must be a book that tells all about it, where I could go to straighten it out in my mind. But I don't know where the book is, and maybe I couldn't read it if I found it.
—Warren G. Harding

I am a man of limited talents from a small town; I don't seem to grasp that I am president.
—G Hard

My God, this is a hell of a job! I have no trouble with my enemies. I can take care of my enemies all right. But my damn friends, my God-damn friends, White, they're the ones that keep me walking the floor nights!
—G Hard

Back in the day, Harding's career got under way with a whimper as he lost in a bid to be governor of Ohio. Some thought he was destined for a life in the newspaper business, but within eleven years he had attained the highest office in the land. Only in America.

Following the conclusion of World War I, Woodrow Wilson faded from the scene and the presidential race was wide open.

Harding had been just vague enough on the League of Nations proposal to avoid offending anyone. He further mastered this mumbling and bumbling technique by sharing noncommittal utterances on the campaign trail, like a rapper lacking confidence in his lyrics and style. Harding never would have received his party's nomination had the media machine been around back in the day.

> I am not fit for this office and should never have been here.
> —G Hard

But America was sold. Harding received 61 percent of the votes, and yet another candidate from The O-Hi-O Yo! could call himself president.[30] He knew what his aides in the "poker cabinet" were pulling, but the media machine was not yet fired up and so it took historians to uncover the graft of his presidency. Many of Harding's appointees, including Secretary of the Interior Albert B. Fall and Attorney General Harry M. Daugherty, were implicated in the Teapot Dome scandal. The Veterans' Bureau, the Office of the Alien Property Custodian, and the departments of the Interior and Justice were also scarred, but Harding died before his good name could be sullied. Merciful treatment by the press and a merciful death, for sure.

85

That death came as a result of excess: G Hard loved his whiskey and he loved to smoke. While doing the aforementioned in a San Francisco hotel room, his brain suffered a blowout (i.e., a cerebral embolism) and that was that. RIP, G.

> I don't know much about Americanism, but it's a damn good word with which to carry an election.
> —G Hard

---

[30] The O-Hi-O Yo! boasts five Republican presidents: Rutherford B. Hayes, James A. Garfield, William McKinley, William Howard Taft, and Warren G. Harding.

> I thought I could swing it . . . I think the American public wants a solemn ass as president and I think I'll go along with them.
> —Calvin Coolidge

Calvin Coolidge was not from the O-Hi-O Yo!, thus the rap comparisons must come to an end. There was no gettin' jiggy for Coolerthanacorpse Coolidge, and even if Snoop Dogg had been one of his aides, I doubt Coolidge would've allowed anyone to *shizzle* his *fizzle*. Bottom line: He was an upright, uptight Puritan and, in many ways, that was what the nation needed after Harding.[31] He quickly threw the riffraff out of the Oval Office—those who hadn't yet been sent up the river—and got down to business. Literally.

The Roaring Twenties were in full swing. Coolidge and Hoover benefited from a GOP-controlled Congress and no one saw any need to be anything less than exuberant. Depression was not the D word of the day. Dancing was. Drinking—albeit, illegal—was. Debauchery was. And as far as Calvin was concerned, out of sight was out of mind. He was fond of napping and fell asleep at the wheel as the nation careened toward depression. Somebody must have clued him in to what was coming as he decided to skip out on the presidency in 1929. Yet another four-and-out-the-door *Elephas maximus*.

Not only did Coolidge bail on the Oval Office, he bailed on his party. So disinterested in maintaining affiliation was Coolidge that he was quoted as saying, "That man has offered me unsolicited advice

> How can they tell?
> —Dorothy Parker, upon hearing that doctors had declared Coolidge deceased

---

[31] The wackiest he got was having a pet pig. Had Benjamin Harrison still been around, there definitely would have been bacon for breakfast.

for six years, most of it bad," when asked about why he wasn't actively endorsing Herbert Hoover. That's cold, Calvin.

Still, some folks are fond of Coolidge and the way he was able to sleepwalk through his presidency. As a matter of fact, the grand poo-bah of voodoo economics, Ronald Reagan, was so inspired that he had a White House portrait of Truman replaced with one of Coolidge. Both Reagan and Coolidge were unsuccessful with their tax-slashing programs, so the respect makes sense.

Coolidge had daydreamed his way through too many economic outlook reports, and, by the time Hoover took office, it was impossible to wake the country from its economic slumber. He just wasn't the leader that the times required. In fact, his wife was more accomplished. Lou Hoover was an academic and an outdoorswoman. She spoke Chinese and Latin and did an impressive amount of charity work during the Great Depression. Unlike her husband.

Under his watch, newspapers would come to be known as "Hoover blankets"; "Hoover flags" were the white of a turned-out pocket ("Sorry, brother. I *don't* have a dime."); and "Hoovervilles" were, of course, the shantytowns of the homeless. The word "Hoover" was on par with any of the day's choicest cusswords.

> When a great many people are unable to find work, unemployment results.[32]
> —Calvin Coolidge, Master of the Obvious!

> Nero fiddled while Rome burned, but Coolidge only snores.
> —H. L. Mencken, on Coolidge's role in the impending depression

---

[32] A ha! So that's how that works! (This was the man who also said, "After all, the chief business of the American people is business.")

87

> I have no fears for the future of our country. It is bright with hope.
> —Herbert Hoover, shortly before the stock market crashed

Like Teddy Bear Roosevelt, Hoover was a conservative convinced that since he'd overcome the odds, everyone else could, too. And if you didn't, you had no one to blame but yourself. Even if there were no jobs to be worked and the bank had taken away your home. Even if your children were starving and you'd give your left arm for a dusty bowl full of food. So impervious was Hoover that when asked about all who'd perished during the Great Depression, he said, "I outlived the bastards."[33]

Hoover's chilly disposition didn't bode well for relationships. One popular story had him asking to borrow a nickel so as to call a friend. The response was, "Here's a dime. Call all your friends." He was such a snob that he ordered all of the servants in the White House to hide—yes, hide!—whenever he walked by. Cooks in the closets . . . butlers in the bushes . . . Failure to do so meant your job; quite a threat, given the times.

> I cannot think offhand of any big-league politicians who were unqualifiedly for Hoover, who really wanted him. Most of them were openly or covertly against him.
> —Alice Roosevelt Longworth, tellin' it like it is

---

[33] It's at times like this that my "hate" borders on legitimate emotion.

During Hoover's presidency, all of Teddy Bear's good work was laid to waste, thus requiring another Roosevelt to come along and fix things up.

WALL STREET LAYS AN EGG
—*Variety* headline after Black Tuesday

Tariffs rose to an all-time high under Hoover, and the Sherman Anti-Trust Act was conveniently forgotten, as companies such as Ford and US Steel dominated their respective markets. They were doing well, as were their stockholders, yet somehow, some way, for some reason, nobody else was benefiting. Dumbo was no longer walking among the people; he was high in the sky, flying above it all and enjoying his limited perspective.

Despite his lack of ideas, the Republicans decided to run Hoover again in 1932. They did so even though his hair had gone completely white since the last convention. They did so even though high school history students would be making "Hoover sucks" jokes for years to come. The GOP ran him because it was what big business wanted. But what big business wanted, for once, big business did not get. FDR was victorious, as Hoover carried just six states. The now-former president slinked home, having been reminded that, à la his name, he sucked. How could he have ever thought otherwise? During this time, the entire Republican approach to the Depression sucked. Sucked, sucked, sucked.

89

Economic depression cannot be cured by legislative action or executive pronouncement.
—Herbert Hoover, shortly before being drop-kicked from office

As further evidence of the party's identity crisis during the 1930s, Republican congressmen were all opposed to getting

> I can say that never in the last fifteen years have I had the peace of mind that I have since the election. I have almost a feeling of elation.
> —Herbert Hoover, shortly after losing the presidential election[34]

involved in Europe's war. Virtual doves, they were known as "Isolationists," a term that hasn't shared headline space with "GOP" since. By 1940, though, the GOP was ready to go international. They nominated Wendell Wilkie on the strength of his pro-war, pro-farmer platform, but FDR took it to him without breaking a sweat. In the lexicon of tough-guy names, Franklin scores much higher than Wendell, and the country—squaring off against Adolf (significantly lower on the scale) Hitler—needed tough.

90

FDR went on to win an unprecedented fourth term in office in 1944, and the U.S. went on to win the war. That sailor went on to kiss that girl in Times Square, and life went on, the calm prosperity of the 1950s replacing the torrid pace of the Roaring Twenties and the desperate death knell of the 1930s and early 1940s. The GOP was reintroduced to itself and, as the Cold War kicked into gear, never again would a Republican plead isolation.

> I cannot conceive of any circumstance that could drag out of me permission to consider me for any political post from dogcatcher to Grand High Supreme King of the Universe.
> —Dwight D. Eisenhower

[34] Sucked!!!

In the 1950s, the world was the GOP's oyster as General Eisenhower enjoyed a resounding victory. But like Truman before him, he did little to quell the Red Scare and for most of the decade, people's rights were infringed upon in a way eerily and ironically similar to the tales told of communist countries.

Speaking of irony, communists were not known just as "Reds." They were often referred to as "Pinkos." Not around Ike, however. His wife, Mamie, loved the color pink and decorated their bedroom as such. That's right, all pink. This surely garnered some jokes: a military man now the leader of the free world and his bedroom was powder-puff pink . . .[35]

Also ironic is the fact that Pink's parents were both pacifists. Actually, their religious beliefs may have played a role in his "atoms for peace" plan. The bomb was Pink's favorite deterrent, a decidedly Republican tactic that would be practiced throughout the Cold War. For sure, as president he was more comfortable with foreign affairs than domestic issues. Pink's cabinet was filled with business executives, and those execs wanted a balanced budget, yet under him there was an astronomical increase in defense spending. Did somebody mention "decidedly Republican tactic?"

Another of Pink's domestic thorns was Senator

> She's pink right down to her underwear.
> —Richard M. Nixon, on congressional opponent Helen Gahagan Douglas

> I just won't get into a pissing contest with that skunk.
> —Dwight D. Eisenhower, referring to McCarthy

91

---

[35] Talk about *Queer Eye for the Straight Guy!*

> Ankles are nearly always neat and good-looking,
> but knees are nearly always not.
> —Pink, discussing the elephant's four knees
> (I think)

Joe McCarthy, whose leash was let out way too long. Not all Republicans agreed with McCarthyism, Pink Ike included, but most kept their mouths shut for fear of recrimination. Ironic, isn't it, given the nature of communism?

So much irony in the time of the Iron Curtain. How ironic.

> Any man who wants to be president is
> either an egomaniac or crazy.
> —Pink

Things are more like they are now
than they ever were before.
—Dwight D. Eisenhower,
doing his Yogi Berra imitation

The Republican Party makes even its young men seem old.
—Adlai Stevenson

Chapter Nine

Adam in the Garden:
Wednesday

"Hellllll-oh!"

"Hey, Apple Cart. You sure sound chipper."

"I'm having the time of my life, Reverend! Up late last night and up early this morning. I walked to the World Trade Center and then down to Battery Park to see Ellis Island and Lady Liberty. She looks so small out there, but all the more amazing because of it. At that height, she's like, eye-level with all of those immigrants who came in on all of those boats. I got chills."

"With all of the foreign languages I hear, sometimes I think Ellis Island is still open."

> The values to which the conservative appeals are inevitably caricatured by the individuals designated to put them into practice.
> —Harold Rosenberg

"The best part was, I talked with so many different people. It wasn't what I'd been warned of at all. This is such a friendly city! The most interesting people, too. All walks of life."

"Go easy on me, chatterbox. Bennett and I went upstate to gamble last night."

"Late night?"

"Yeah."

"Well then, that makes two of us!"

"I didn't get to make any acting connections, but—"

"You're in the wrong party for that, Reverend Tom."

"—but, there were a couple of bigwigs with us. Mitch McConnell and Bill Frist came along for the ride."

"That's cool."

"It was a great trip, but the ride home was hell. Those two wouldn't know shut up if it hit them square in the face! Oh, the plans they have: casinos in every state, with Bennett's slot machines and everything, soft money loopholes, a morning-after pill but no abortion, a new-look tax package. I'm glad to know I've got guys like that at the helm; guys who eat, breathe, and sleep Republicanism. I'm paying for it today, though."

> Twelve dollars for a movie ticket. Now that's a sin!
> —David Letterman's "Top Ten Comments Overheard at *The Passion of the Christ*"

"You win any money?"

"Not really."

"Ha! It's a yes or no question, Reverend."

"What do *you* know about casinos, Apple Cart?"

"Not much. I can't imagine the good Lord cares much for them, though. But I've got a joke to make you feel better . . . A guy from my church at home emailed it to me. There was a tragedy today in Iraq. Did you hear about it? A Jeep ran over a box of popcorn . . . and killed ten kernels!"

"Wow. You *are* country."

"Thank you. Thank you! Now, can we get down to business? I went to a forum called 'Religion and the Republic' today and, all kidding aside, it really made me mad. The first part was on the impact of Mel Gibson. That was no big deal, but then they got into halting abortion, blurring the separation of church and state, and then all this angry talk about gay priests and gay marriage."

> Did you ever notice the people who are most adamantly against abortions are people so ugly you wouldn't want to touch them in the first place?
> —George Carlin

97

> They've entered into the arena on the side of evil, and we pray, oh God, that you might raise a standard against them.
> —Pat Robertson, after Texas's anti-sodomy law was struck down[36]

---

[36] Robertson has used mass prayer to try and "induce" these justices to retire. And yet he accuses feminists of witchcraft . . .

> Gay people should be allowed to get married. Just because somebody's gay doesn't mean he shouldn't suffer like the rest of us!
> —Jeff Shaw

"And?"

"And none of it sat well with me. I went because I didn't think the two R's should be put together like that. You know, 'religion' and 'Republic.' And I walked out more angry than when I walked in. Less confused but more ticked off."

"You're supposed to graduate from college with a trade and some moral fiber, Apple Cart."

"Well, one out of two isn't bad."

"Funny."

"Seriously, I remember being really bummed out when Matthew Shepard was murdered. I was so upset over the idea of him dying alone. I still am upset . . . Besides that, I got to know a couple of gay guys at school and even one woman who's a lesbian."

"Mmmmm, lesbian!"

"Reverend . . ."

"Sorry."

"It's just that the Republican platform seems totally antiquated on these issues."

"I disagree, but go on."

"So, you really think that being gay *isn't* okay?"

"Not even a distant cousin to okay."

"But that war is necessary?"

"More often than not."

"And that tax breaks for big business will really boost the economy and trickle down to the people?"

"Well . . . yeah. Sure."

"And that by-the-book piety is more than being truly, deeply happy?"

"If it's 'happy' as in *gay*, then yes. Yes I do."

"You sound a lot like my dad, Reverend. But I just don't know anymore . . ."

"Do not forsake thy father, Adam. And don't embrace deviant lifestyles just because it's the in-thing to do. Gay is wrong. It's immoral. Marriage was intended to be between a man and a woman. Case closed."

"I know President Bush agrees with you, but I don't know if I agree with him."

"Him or *Him?*"

"Either. That's why I've been struggling so much with this lately. But then I think about all of the Episcopal churches that approve of homosexuality. So . . ."

"The pseudo-Episcopalians, Apple Cart. Like the guys who got their collar through the mail. Stay away from them. They're bad news."

"But you did pretty much the same, didn't you, Tom?"

"Reverend Tom."

"Reverend Tom."

"Something just occurred to me, Adam. You're not one of *them*, are you?"

"Do you promise the seal of confession is in effect even though this is Madison Square Garden?"

"Of course. Wake me with your sins, Apple Cart!"

Most of us enjoy preaching and I've got such a bully pulpit!
—Theodore Roosevelt

You are no more or less a child of God like everyone else . . . What a joy it is to have you here.
—Reverend Douglas Theuner, welcoming Gene Robinson[37]

99

---

[37] The first-ever homosexual bishop of the New Hampshire Episcopalian Diocese.

> Whether we see ourselves as traditional or progressive in our views about sexuality, we may not, in the end, have very much of a say over how our children will handle this aspect of their lives . . . In the end they choose.
> —Jean Jacobs Speizer

"Well then, I am, Reverend Tom. I'm gay as they come."

"Jesus . . . What're we going to do with you? Your poor father. Your poor mother."

"I figure my dad can ask Dick Cheney for advice. I mean, even Bill O'Reilly said we have bigger things to worry about than gay marriage. He called Jerry Falwell and Pat Robertson 'the Christian Taliban.' That cracked me up!"

"Blasphemy! Not only are you gay, you're irreverent. And the only thing worse than gay is irreverent! You're signing a deal with the devil, you know."

"But Reverend, this is my time of need."

"Adam, we're done. I just don't think there's anything more for us to talk about."

"You might be right . . ."

"I doubt I'll be available tomorrow night. You know, with the big speeches and all."

"That's too bad."

"Yep. Too bad."

"I've learned a lot from you this week, Reverend. I really have."

"Good. I'm glad . . . Listen, Apple Cart, I took a real beating at blackjack last

> IT'S ADAM AND EVE, NOT ADAM AND STEVE.
> —Protest sign

night is all. I don't want to give up on you. That's not why I became a man of God. I'll be here before the speeches. I owe it to you and your folks. Since it'll be a special trip, though, I'll need twenty dollars. Actually, thirty dollars, since you seem to have forgotten to pay last night. But most importantly, I need you to remember what Wittgenstein said: 'A confession has to be a part of your new life.' If that's something you're ready to work on, your new life, then come and see me. But if you're not ready to go straight, if you're not ready to dedicate your life to the Republicans and to the church, to your father and mother, if you're not ready to pay your way in this world, namely those thirty beans I just mentioned, well then don't bother me. Go straight to Hell, do not pass go, do not collect two hundred dollars."

"Well, gee, sounds like this buttercup has some thinking to do, huh?"

"Yes you do, my little femme."

"All righty, then. Thanks, Reverend Mark."

"Tom."

"Tom."

"Right."

"Riiiiight."

"You make me want to smoke, Apple Cart. You're some piece of work."

"I'll take that as a compliment."

There is a holy mistaken zeal in politics,
as well as in religion. By persuading others,
we convince ourselves.
—Junius

Dear Lord,

I think my life is really taking shape, right here in the Big Apple. And to think, it took the Republican National Convention to show me the way! Irony, irony, irony . . .

I get along decently with guys like my dad and Tom, but I know what they stand for. I know how dead-set they are against gay rights, affirmative action, preserving forest- land, funding for schools, and anything else I agree with. I apologize for talking to you about politics, but my confes- sionals haven't provided any relief whatsoever. I got more out of that hip hop club and the falafel . . .

Speaking of which, I'm going out with those guys again tonight. They work security at the Garden and have to be the funniest, most interesting people I've ever met. I'm sure we'll have fun and I can't wait! It's me, eyes wide open, Lord, and I know I'm not alone. Everybody is iron- ing it out for themselves. Sanding down the rough edges. In my case now, it's fine sandpaper and not the rougher, coarser stuff like I needed before.

The last conversation we all had last night was about the death penalty and all the poor people that're on death row. This one guy was saying how they're all minority men, too. The Dirty South couldn't be any further removed from Montana, so it was a real education for me. And it isn't just the Dirty South, Lord. How can I feel good about the death penalty after all of the mistakes that were made in Illinois? The answer is . . . I can't.

On the lighter side, we were laughing about Bush and all his talk about going to Mars. Words just can't describe how unimportant that trip is compared to the other issues on the table. One guy said it makes sense because Dubya is comfortable with foreign policy and it doesn't get any more foreign than Mars!

Lord, I'd like to help Tom the way he's trying to help me, the same way all of those confessionals are supposed to help. I think that might be why I'm planning on going back tomorrow night. Plus, I wouldn't feel right leaving without saying good-bye. My mother didn't raise me that way. On that note, thank you for all that you have given me. Mom, Dad, and especially my first New York City bagel. It really helped with my hangover this morning! Time to go out now. See ya!

103

Money for jobs and housing, not war.
It's not a photo-op, George.
—Signs held by protesters at
Martin Luther King, Jr.'s grave[38]

Republicans are the party that says government doesn't work, and then get elected and prove it.
—P. J. O'Rourke

---

[38] Bush won less than 10 percent of the African-American vote in 2000.

Chapter Ten

Republican Anagrams:
An Email Attachment

Two-thirds of the way through the book now, I think we can all agree that my sources have provided fantastic information, from the vertically challenged buckeyes of the Gilded Age to the George Carlin and P. J. O'Rourke quotes. It still bothers me, though, the way I was snubbed by all of those conservative think tanks. Well, I did get one noteworthy response . . .

Dear Mr. Howe,

Thank you for your correspondence. At this time, we are not interested in participating in your research. The AWB is solely dedicated to preserving truth, justice, and the almighty dollar. However, we wish you all the best with your work.

Democratically yours,
Accountants Without Borders

Standard boilerplate, but the noteworthiness came as I discovered an attachment inadvertently included with the email. Much to my surprise, when I opened the document it was a joke that one of the AWB Fellows had written on July 6, 2004, the one hundred fiftieth anniversary of the GOP. In a spoof of the Defense Department code breakers of the early twentieth century, this bean counter turned the names of several prominent Republicans into anagrams.[39] Many of these word scrambles were less than flattering; they poked fun at the very leaders the AWB supports with its models, risk assessment, and other such financial services.

The list from this attachment reads as follows:

- George Bush = *He bugs Gore*
- George Tenet = *get teen ogre*
- Schwarzenegger = *Czar Egg Her News*
- Rush Limbaugh = *him a grub lush*
- Robert Dole = *elder robot*
- Pat Robertson = *protest baron*
- George H. W. Bush = *beg Howe shrug*[40]
- Ronald Reagan = *a granola nerd, arranged loan*, or *Anal Dr. Orange*

---

[39] Who says these think tank guys aren't dedicated to bettering mankind?
[40] I find the presence of my last name to be quite disconcerting . . .

- Gerald Ford = *Lord Rag Fed*
- Tricky Dick = *Dick Tricky*
- Strom Thurmond = *STD month rumor*
- Eisenhower = *weiner shoe*
- Herbert Hoover = *he be vet horror*
- Calvin Coolidge = *cool vigil dance*
- Teddy Roosevelt = *severely odd tot*
- William McKinley = *ye will mimic klan*
- William Taft = *limit fat law*
- Chester Arthur = *truth scare her*
- Rutherford Hayes = *red fresh hurt, yo*
- Ulysses S. Grant = *gassy sent slur*
- Abraham Lincoln = *NAMBLA oral chin*

So, I take it back: There was at least one conservative think tank willing to contribute to the fun that is *Why I Hate the Republicans!*

"Paging *Dr. Anal Orange* . . . *Dr. Anal Orange* . . . You're needed in proctology, stat. *Dr. Anal Orange* . . ."

I would have made a good Pope.
—Richard M. Nixon

Chapter Eleven

Elephas Maximus: From Dick Tricky to King George II

In 1960, Richard Nixon battled John F. Kennedy in a race close enough to make 2000 look like a landslide. Hollywood can make or break a career, and nobody likes a sweaty president. Thus, Nixon had to wait a few years before ascending to the Oval Office. In the interim, he learned to make use of the TV. Antiperspirant, too.

You can't blame the guy for being so nervous on camera. It wasn't like he came highly recommended or anything. Nope, one issue that the two parties could agree on was *Dick Tricky.* "If you give me one week, I might think of one. I don't remember," said Eisenhower when asked about the contributions of his vice president. "Nixon is a shifty, goddamn liar, and people know it," said Harry S. Truman. Wow. This is like the worst Get Well Never card I've ever read. After Nixon

> Let us understand:
> North Vietnam cannot
> defeat or humiliate the
> United States. Only
> Americans can do that.
> —*Dick Tricky*

proved them all right with Watergate, the accolades continued to flow. "I mean, there's a smell to it. Let's get rid of that smell." This was Barry Goldwater (*try gal wardrobe*), in 1973. He'd certainly had enough. Author William S. Burroughs added, "I think that Richard Nixon will go down in history as a true folk hero, who struck a vital blow to the whole diseased concept of the revered image and gave the American virtue of irreverence and skepticism back to the people." Folk hero . . . Now there's a nice way of cloaking the dagger.

Even Nixon speechwriter Pat Buchanan (*NAACP ban hut*) chipped in: "The president is no longer a credible custodian of the conservative political tradition of the GOP." *Au contraire*, Patrick. I think he exemplifies to a T the conservative tradition!

But before all that nasty business, there was 1968 and *Dick Tricky* sneaking into office through the servant's entrance. He took the presidency with a grand total of 38 percent of the popular vote. He won by appealing to the "silent majority" on a platform of "law and order." "Silent" as in erased tapes? "Law and order" as in a vice president only slightly less criminal than

110

> Agnew was involved in several conspiracies in Maryland that included bribery, tax fraud, and extortion. He had been taking payments and kickbacks from state contractors. These arrangements continued once he became vice president.
> —Lewis L. Gould

the president himself? You just can't make this stuff up.

With all of the misguided espionage, there was hardly time to get anything meaningful done. Especially when you factor in how much work it would take if *Dick Tricky* were to be reelected.

Since the days of Reconstruction, the GOP had been desperately trying to figure out a way to woo white Southern males. With their votes, DC dominance would be assured. So, Nixon did what he felt he had to do: his strategy, in regards to the Third Coast, the Dirty South, was to weaken the federal government's commitment to racial equality. Of affirmative action, he said, "With blacks you can usually settle for an incompetent, because there are just not enough competent ones." America would have been offended by the lying alone, but *Dick Tricky* far exceeded expectations, spewing sound bites and covert directives that went from the sublime to the ridiculous.

What politicians don't understand is that people are genuinely offended when lied to. It comes across as condescending. And there is nothing more bloodthirsty than a mob that's been condescended to.

Watergate was not to be the only test of *Dick Tricky's* deodorant. His rap sheet included illegal campaign donations—Yankees owner George Steinbrenner was given a severe spanking for his contribution—not to mention the kickbacks his vice president took. And then there's Checkers. Presidents love their dogs, and Nixon was no exception. The cocker spaniel had been given to him amidst a donor scandal, and there were calls for Checkers's return. So strongly did Nixon feel about his pooch that he argued his case on national TV. Apparently, he now under-

When the President does it, that means that it's not illegal.
—*Dick Tricky*

111

Don't you dare call me Dick.
—*Dick Tricky*,
to an aide

> The more you stay in this kind of job, the more you realize that a public figure, a major public figure, is a lonely man.
> —Richard M. Nixon[41]

stood what the boob tube was for, just not how he should use it as president of the United States.

Of course, Watergate would far surpass his "Checkers Speech." In 1972, Attorney General John Mitchell made reference to the "White House horrors" as Woodward and Bernstein's investigations began to gain credibility. In that same year Nixon would be re-elected with a much-improved 43 percent of the popular vote, but the end was near. On the bright side, he still had Checkers.

When Spiro Agnew (*a new GOP, sir!*) resigned, Nixon saw the writing on the wall. He knew he could be next, so he did what any good politician would do: he chose a vice president nobody'd ever, ever want to see in the Oval Office. He chose Jerry Ford.

Upon taking over from Dick Tricky, Ford said, "I assume the presidency under extraordinary circumstances . . . This is an hour of history that troubles our minds and hurts our hearts." But once the cameras were off and he'd loosened his tie, he joked, "Richard Nixon was just offered two million dollars by Schick to do a television commercial—for Gillette!"

He kicked off his Hush Puppies and quipped, "If Lincoln were alive today, he'd be turning over in his

> I've had a lot of experience with people smarter than I am.
> —Gerald Ford, aka *Rag Fed Lord*

[41] And Sting sings: "All made up and nowhere to go, welcome to this one-man show. So lonely, so lonely, so lonely."

112

grave." Nixon was gone, but Yogi Berra (*I orgy bare*) Ford was now our commander in chief.

Despite doing well at Yale Law School and making a life for himself in politics, other Fordian Yogi-isms followed. Athletic aphorisms like, "I watch a lot of baseball on the radio." Actions speak louder than words, but this is the same man who locked himself out of the White House one night, while walking his dog, Liberty! Lyndon B. Johnson accused Ford of playing football for too long without a helmet. I'm not sure if this was before or after he said Ford couldn't walk and fart at the same time. But I suppose it isn't really the chronology that matters.

The fact that the unelected president was often dazed and confused should not be surprising. You'd be a little discombobulated, too, if somebody changed your name at four years of age. When Leslie Lynch King Jr.'s mother remarried, her new husband saw fit to not only adopt her son, he decided to (re)name the kid after himself. Thus, in 1917, Leslie King became Gerald Rudolph Ford, future president of the United States. A reborn Republican!

To add to Leslie-turned-Jerry's confusion, he got to be president without ever being elected. He was the first and only president to attain office in this manner, having been named by Nixon to the office

> I guess it just proves that in America anyone can be president.
> —Gerald Ford

> Obviously, it's a great privilege and pleasure to be here at the Yale Law School Sesquicentennial Convocation. And I defy anyone to say that and chew gum at the same time.
> —Gerald Ford

> When a man is asked to make a speech, the first thing he has to decide is what to say.
> —Gerald Ford, with another Yogi-ism

of vice president, post-Agnew, and then movin' on up like George and Weezie when *Dick Tricky* resigned. He was the leader of the free world without ever appearing on a ticket. In 1976, he'd get his chance. And after just 895 days in the White House he would blow that chance.[42]

Part of the problem was that on an otherwise pleasant Sunday morning in 1974, Ford had pardoned Nixon. A skeptical public took this as another slap in the face, and the GOP would spend years trying to make the Democrats seem equally immoral. Hooking up with the religious right and bashing Bill Clinton—who'd also experienced a post-divorce name change as a boy—would be among those feeble efforts.

Speaking of feeble efforts, there really is no other way to describe the effort that the GOP has made on behalf of impoverished minorities. When Strom Thurmond and the Ku Klux Klan (a name without one single anagram . . .) began to support Republican candidates, it was a reminder to mainstream America that the nation was not yet free from prejudice. The fact that it continues today is more disconcerting than a Janet Jackson wardrobe malfunction.

The 1964 election was significant for the Republicans not because they won—which they didn't—but because Barry Goldwater indoctrinated Reagan in the ways of *Elephas maximus*. When

---

[42] According to the *Congressional Quarterly,* Ford was, "a man more comfortable carrying out the programs of others than in initiating things on his own."

> I know I am getting better at golf because I am hitting fewer spectators.
> —Gerald Foooore!d

I would hope that understanding
and reconciliation are not limited to the 19th
hole alone.
—*Rag Fed Lord*, getting deep

A blue ribbon panel headed by former
presidents Gerald Ford and Jimmy Carter came up
with a list of ways to improve the next presidential
election. Are these the best guys for the job?
I mean, between the two of them,
they could only win one election.
—Jay Leno

He was one of the few political leaders I have
ever met whose public speeches revealed more
than his private conversations.
—*Rag Fed Lord*, discussing *Anal Dr. Orange*

Goldwater said, "Extremism in the defense of liberty is no vice. And let me remind you that moderation in the pursuit of justice is no virtue," Reagan was listening.

In a nutshell, by 1962 Reagan was caught up, hook, line, and sinker, in George Kennan's notion of containment; a notion Kennan would later refute. On top of that, he was tired of paying taxes on his

> It's true hard work
> never killed anybody,
> but I figure, why take
> the chance?
> —Ronald Reagan

Tinsel Town take. So, he decided to become a Republican.[43] And like any new cult member, he went overboard. He didn't just sip the Kool-Aid; he chugged it! On his agenda was neutering the Soviet Union and tightening the national belt. His fiscal policies earned a number of nicknames over the years, most notably "Reaganomics" and "voodoo economics." The latter came compliments of his own vice president, George H. W. Bush. Others referred to Reagan's bare-bones style as "root canal economics." Reduce taxes, *Dr. Anal Orange,* and hold the Novocain . . .

Reagan simply referred to his plan as "supply side economics." Although he would argue otherwise, this basically meant supplying military contractors with huge contracts and providing big business with big tax breaks. Eventually, billions and billions were supposed to trickle their way down to the secretaries and steel workers, the teamsters and the teachers. The trickle wasn't to be, though; not like those Roman aqueducts. Only the proverbial elephant dung made its way south hitting the fan or, in some cases, the propeller.[44] A house divided cannot stand, and the division between rich and poor widened significantly during the 1980s.

As the Soviet people waited in line for bread and toilet paper, our ballistic missile count rose faster than John Candy's bad cholesterol.

> I didn't leave the
> Democratic Party.
> The Democratic
> Party left me.
> —Ronald Reagan,
> confusing his former
> party with, with . . .

116

---

[43] Before cashing in on *Bonzo,* he'd been satisfied to act as president of the Screen Actors Guild. When the paychecks really started to flow, though, he aspired to higher heights.

[44] See "air traffic controllers' strike."

The whole aim of practical politics is to keep the populace in a continual state of alarm (and hence clamorous to be led to safety) by menacing them with an endless series of hobgoblins, all of them imaginary.
—H. L. Mencken

We're in greater danger today than we were the day after Pearl Harbor. Our military is absolutely incapable of defending this country.
—Ronald Reagan, in an advertisement for *Fear Factor*

Reagan claimed not to know a thing about the Iran-Contra scandal and the majority of Americans decided to let him off as an aging, doddering delegator. If that isn't the performance of a lifetime, what is?
—Cormac O'Brien

Americans waited in lines of their own: mainly unemployment lines. The national debt doubled during Reagan's tenure, just like spending on defense. Was it external pressure that brought down the Berlin Wall? Or was it long overdue implosion? I know how Reagan remembers it.

Whatever it is that the government does, sensible Americans would prefer that the government do it to somebody else. This is the idea behind foreign policy.
—P. J. O'Rourke

He remembers his famous line, the one that Colin Powell and the rest of the Defense Department tried to get him to cut. But, Reagan opted to ride in on his white horse: "Mr. Gorbachev, tear down this wall." Methinks it was coming down anyway, Ronnie.

But before that famous day in 1989, Reagan made sure that there was some side action going on—you know, just in case that defense budget wasn't big enough. So, *Arranged Loan* improvised some military contracts of his own. When news of the Iran-Contra Affair broke, *Arranged Loan* and Big Daddy Bush were caught with their pants down. Literally. Reagan played unaware because what else does a president do when the dirty laundry is exposed? Big Daddy simply claimed to have been in the bathroom when the deal was discussed with go-between Oliver North.

The nation watched as North took his oath. Goldwater had schooled Reagan in conservatism and Reagan returned the favor, teaching North all he knew about being a thespian.[45]

Continuing the tradition of out-fund-raising the Democrats, Reagan's Republicans shamed Carter to the tune of $77 million versus $16 million in 1980. (That's a lot of jelly beans and not nearly enough peanuts.) GOP supporters everywhere pitched their pennies in for the Gipper, and it meant plenty of nickels and dimes in return. They turned out in

---

[45] Calm yourselves, religious right wingers. "Thespian" is simply another word for "actor."

I don't know if I could do this job if I weren't an actor.
—The Gipper

force, once again, in 1984. Reagan played the part just as they scripted it for him, keeping taxes down for the upper crust and throwing around corporate tax breaks like they were bananas for Bonzo.

> Unemployment insurance is a prepaid vacation for freeloaders.
> —Ronald Reagan

By the time he left office, though, Reagan's days of acting were over. His brain had slowly been turning to applesauce, earliest evidence being his lack of coherence on the '84 campaign trail. "The Great Communicator" sounded like a punch-drunk Muhammad Ali, just with less focus and purpose.[46] As soon as he passes away, look for Reagan's likeness to replace FDR on the dime. And hey, why not? Plenty of people had to ask, "Brother, can you spare a dime?" during his presidency, so sure, go right ahead if it makes you feel better. In the age of debit and credit cards, it's really, really, really important that we change who appears on our change. While these obviously very busy folks are at it, they should go for broke and knock their first hero off the penny, as well; replace him with King George II. Lincoln won't mind. He's dead.

The crowned prince of Kennebunkport on the penny . . . A fitting monument, seeing as his tax refund put no more than a few pennies in our pockets. That's economic recovery, Republican-style.

Before moving on to Bush, let's talk trees. Most Republicans have voting records that place them on the environmental Most Wanted list, but Reagan was tops. Teddy Roosevelt would thwack him and King George II with his big stick if he were still alive today. During his years in office, never was *A Granola Nerd's* obtuseness more obvious than on environmental issues.

---

[46] And this was ten years before the Alzheimer's supposedly kicked in.

> We should declare war on North Vietnam. . . .
> We could pave the whole country and put parking
> strips on it, and still be home by Christmas.
> —Ronald Reagan

For example, he told *Sierra* magazine that, "Approximately 80 percent of our air pollution stems from hydrocarbons released by vegetation, so let's not go overboard in setting and enforcing tough emission standards from man-made sources." Good thing McDonald's is cutting down so much of the Brazilian rain forest then. And then this gem, in the *Sacramento Bee:* "A tree's a tree. How many more do you need to look at?" I think it's safe to say that this granola nerd was no tree hugger. And no friend to hippies, either. Back when he was governor of California, during the summer of love, he said, "They act like Tarzan, look like Jane, and smell like Cheetah." I wonder what his advice is to Arnold Schwarzenegger on the gay couples flocking to San Francisco to get married. I bet you they're coming up with some good nicknames at this very moment. Of course, between granola brain and the Austrian Agitator, these names probably sound like bad anagrams, but that's just this guy's opinion.

If Bush wins, I'm moving to Canada.

> We're the party that wants to see an America in
> which people can still get rich.[47]
> —Ronald Reagan

---

[47] Again, the number fifty-five (that's how many people got rich under Reagan).

Well, I learned a lot. . . . You'd be surprised.
They're all individual countries.
—Ronald Reagan, after a tour of South America

Abortion is advocated only by persons who have
themselves been born.
—Ronald Reagan, proving that
Pro Lifers were hatched from eggs

Government's view of the economy could be
summed up in a few short phrases:
If it moves, tax it. If it keeps moving, regulate it.
And if it stops moving, subsidize it.
—Ronald Reagan[48]

I have strong reservations about George Bush. I'm
concerned about turning the country over to him.
—Ronald Reagan

---

[48] If the economy has stopped moving and you give tax refunds, isn't that the same as subsidizing? A
rose by any other name would smell as stankonia!

> Bush had trouble connecting with women voters. The gag was that he reminded every woman of her first husband.
> —Lewis L. Gould

It was in 1988 that this Great White North reference first became a part of pop culture. And it was in 1989 that interest in curling, maple leaves, and Bob and Doug MacKenzie spiked.

But first things first. To show that Big Daddy Bush is capable of surrounding himself with some Canadian-style hijinks, let's revisit one of the nicknames he had in his younger days. As an anti-abortion congressman in the 1960s, he was actually called "Rubbers" by his peers. Rubbers!!! Ironic, then, that his party would make sure that AIDS and teen pregnancy flourished as publicly funded institutions that distributed condoms and provided family planning were cut off at the knees—even in the midst of his "thousand points of light" plea for help. Where that light was supposed to come from, I do not know, but I suspect that Nancy Reagan and her astrologists were consulted.

Reagan's war on drugs was also waged under Big Daddy Bush. Like Iraq, this war is still being waged today. All along, "Just Say No" has needed a Young & Rubicam face-lift. (Just ask the Reagan and Bush kids. Ask King George II himself. Sniff! Sniff!) The GOP usually pays such close attention to issues abroad—when will they realize that the drug war must also be fought on foreign soil?

> Nobody saves America by sniffing cocaine,
> Jiggling yr knees blankeyed in the rain,
> When it snows in yr nose you catch cold in yr brain.
> —Allen Ginsberg

> The unpleasant sound Bush is emitting as he traipses from one conservative gathering to another is a thin, tinny "arf"—the sound of a lap dog.
> —George Will

Enough Fat Cats and their First Ladies have popped pills and slugged back booze to know that once addiction sinks its teeth in, the user becomes a victim and not a criminal. Why didn't the Kings George consult Betty Ford rather than Nancy Reagan? DARE, "Just Say No," and initiatives like mandatory sentencing have yet to produce the desired results. I thought this was supposed to be the age of accountability?

Big Daddy Bush's crowning moment was beating back Iraq in the Persian Gulf War. The Kuwaitis bestowed upon him a hero's wreath; he got to ride the symbolic white horse into the winner's circle. Vice President Danforth Quayle (*Qatar, hold ye fun!*) was given a My Little Pony. The victory was bittersweet, though; a job half done and a job that left the Kurdish people half dead. Saddam wreaked havoc on them as well as the Shi'ites in the South.[49] They'd been promised support if they revolted. Instead, Big Daddy pulled an invasion interruptus. As questions arose about our place in the Middle East, many a Republican was called out on the carpet for shirking his duties in Vietnam. Those who had failed to serve honorably, yet were gung ho about the war against Iraq, were dubbed "chicken hawks." That's almost as funny as "Rubbers."

Here's another light fact to keep the ball rolling. After Big Daddy Bush puked on his host, the prime minister of Japan, a new colloquialism was welcomed into the Japanese language: *Bushu suru*

123

---

[49] It isn't just in the U.S. that a house divided cannot stand . . .

> Senator, I served with Jack Kennedy, I knew Jack Kennedy . . . You are no Jack Kennedy.
> —Lloyd Bentsen, responding to Dan Quayle

("do a Bush") is now the hip phrase for vomiting![50] Oh, Rubbers . . . Whatever are we going to do with you?

Speaking of wanting to puke, the 1990s were, at least for a while, the era of Newt. From one Persian Gulf War to the next, the Republican chicken hawk brigade has included such notables as Newt Gingrich, George W. Bush and his sidekick Dick ("I had other priorities during the 1960s . . .") Cheney, Dan Quayle, and Rush Limbaugh. Rush seems to have failed in all sorts of wars, military and drug included.

Everybody knows how often Mr. Potatoe Head mumbled and fumbled while assisting Big Daddy Bush, but here's something he did right (at least in the GOP's eyes). Following in Reagan's footsteps, he showed a real ability to build the war chest; he had a dexterity for the dollars, that boy did. For some reason, old coots and corporations alike felt compelled to throw thousands of dollars his way. Maybe Mr. Potatoe Head looked like he could be easily bought. Maybe he came across as too dumb to welch on promises. Maybe it was the fact that

> What a waste it is to lose one's mind. Or not to have a mind is being very wasteful. How true that is.
> —Dan Quayle, speaking to members of the United Negro College Fund[51]

---

[50] Somewhere, Snoop Dogg is jealous.

[51] Quayle was known as "Mr. Potatoe Head" after making a spelling mistake at an elementary school. Potatoe, potato, tomatoe, tomato, let's call the whole thing off!

124

Boy, they were big on crematoriums, weren't they?
—Big Daddy Yogi *Bushu suru,*
during a tour of Auschwitz!

I have opinions of my own, strong opinions, but I
don't always agree with them.
—Big Daddy Bush, paying tribute to Gerald
"Yogi" Ford

I stand for anti-bigotry, anti-Semitism, and
anti-racism.
—George "Yogi" Bush

125

We're enjoying sluggish times and not enjoying
them very much.
—"Yogi" Bush

I'm not what you call your basic intellectual.
—Yogi Bush[52]

---

[52] And by now, even Yogi is getting offended.

> This is not about a bigger welfare state or a cheaper welfare state. This is about replacing a system that is killing our children.
> —Newt Gingrich

he was handsome in that 1980s, *Miami Vice*, brush-cut style. Espadrilles, anyone?

And so Big Daddy Bush let Quayle stay on the ticket in 1992. The decision would prove costly, but the stage was set for 2000 when the First Family would return to their House.

So Bill Clinton took office, but the Republicans still had a few tricks up their sleeve. In 1994, they gained control over both houses of Congress (the first time this had happened for them since 1954) and, riding that tide of confidence, they decided to let their Newt slime his way around Foggy Bottom. They allowed him to grab center stage; to introduce himself and his agenda to the country. Although he looked a bit like Phil Donahue, Newt was anything but congenial. And unlike the better talk show hosts, he wasn't a big fan of letting other people talk.

Newt Gingrich (*rich gent wing*) was very proud of his "Contract with America," an ultraconservative list of proposals that was supposed to reshape the congressional agenda. Fortunately, Newt was so blustery that he blew out his own fuse, but the fact that the GOP would let him go on for so long is scary. Then again, this is the party that let the leash out on Joe McCarthy.

Clinton served his eight years, surviving Ken Starr's GOP Gestapo hunt, and then handed the reins over to Al Gore. Democrats

> This was the most poorly planned and executed incumbent presidential campaign in this century.
> —Dan Quayle, after he and Big Daddy lost in 1992

> It is impossible to maintain civilization with twelve-year-olds having babies, fifteen-year-olds killing each other, seventeen-year-olds dying of AIDS, and eighteen-year-olds receiving diplomas they cannot read.
> —Newt Gingrich, right before arguing for education and social welfare cuts[53]

everywhere rejoiced when the Republicans picked the crowned prince of Kennebunkport as their great white hope. Little did the country know that he would soon be king.

When he was a mere prince, Dubya flew for the Texas Air National Guard and then requested a transfer to Alabama so that he could do some campaigning for a friend of his father's. The problem is, only one Guardsman remembers ever seeing him report for duty. Even if he did, there is the little matter of his entrance exam, back

> The press, which had probed every aspect of the lives of the Clintons, largely accepted George W. Bush at his own evaluation of himself and made only sporadic inquiries into his background and character.
> —Lewis L. Gould, recognizing that not all media is liberal

---

[53] I really did hate Newt Gingrich.

> People never lie so much as after a hunt, during a war, or before an election.
> —Otto von Bismarck, German Chancellor

in Texas. Nobody's ever confused the crowned prince with a rocket scientist, but how does a Yale grad score in the twenty-fifth percentile? And the bigger question is . . . How does he score so poorly and still get accepted, leapfrogging all of the other guys hoping to avoid Vietnam?[54] Dubya would be rewarded for all of his hard work with an honorable discharge. This was a mind not to be wasted; he was destined for Harvard, after all. The first president with an MBA, the crowned prince of Kennbunkport showed little business sense while at school and this continued once he entered the working world. Investors hoped to curry favor with Big Daddy Bush, so they signed on when the vice president's son came calling. He would then bail before the bottom fell out of the business, turning a nice little profit. Similarly, the Texas Rangers made it to the playoffs a few times, lost to the Yankees, and were sent back to the Lone Star State with their *Elephas* tails between their legs. It was the best they'd ever done in their history and the best they'd ever do. Right after one particular Juan Gonzalez home run, Dubya sold his shares and became governor of Texas, recalling, in his campaign speeches, his time in the Texas Air National Guard. Or was that the Alabama National Guard? Shucks, I just can't seem to remember . . . Laura, where's my magic belt buckle?

Perhaps we should be thankful he didn't serve in Vietnam. After all, do we really want a guy willing to stab The Terminator in the

---

[54] The crowned prince was also arrested once and cited for several driving infractions, including driving under the influence, before being accepted into the National Guard. This information was magically deleted from his record as it would have meant application . . . denied.

back out in the fields? I am still perplexed by his decision to grant illegal immigrants citizenship. It is such an about-face, especially for a Republican who used to be the governor of a border state. A moment of thought provides the answer: What does King George II care about Arnie's campaign promises when he's got his own election to win?

King George II has no love of the open-door policy, but he'd rather welcome immigrants than work on his résumé. Many think, and rightly so, that this decision is mere strategy to garner Hispanic support on Election Day. Cecilia Munoz of the National Council of La Raza called Bush's tactic "Piñata Politics." Even Arnie is beginning to suspect, I suspect, that come January 2005, King George II will be saying, "Hasta la vista, baby!"

The shift is already on. When King George II's job approval rating dropped ten points in January of 2004—after David Kay's report was released—he took the news in stride. Word is, he did his best Martha Stewart (*wrest a ham tart*) impersonation, screaming at Karl Rove to, "Sell! Sell!! Sell!!!" Later that night, Lemonade Laura, the loquacious librarian, sternly informed him that there are no holdings or options when you are the president; just reputation, reelection, and historians to act as judge, jury, and board of directors. At that point, he began to cry, "Daddy! Daddy!! Daddy!!!"

"We're obviously looking forward to when the president starts getting into campaign mode," King George II's chief strategist, Matthew Dowd, said in response to continued criticism. From fund-raising mode to "campaign mode". . . What ever happened to representing-the-people mode?

Four years has passed quickly, with the usual GOP calamities: war, unemployment, constituencies offended, and

> Every immigrant who comes here should be required within five years to learn English or leave the country.
> —Theodore Roosevelt

civil rights suspended; the president's rating plummeting faster than ImClone (*con mile*) stock on that fateful day. Unfortunately, the nation's economy did not show the resilience of ImClone, and King George II is going down faster than the matronly Martha before a vegan jury. He may be full of bull, but under his watch, the market has been all bear. Don't worry: I'm sure that King George II will figure out a way to turn this into personal gain. It's just that none of us should count on a share of the profit.

The U.S. budget is out of control. Any thoughts of relief thereafter are a pipe dream until political priorities adjust.
—Goldman, Sachs & Co. in a letter to its clients

The numbers are astonishing. Congress is now spending money like a drunken sailor. And I've never known a sailor drunk or sober with the imagination that this Congress has.

—Senator John McCain (R-AZ)

Chapter Twelve

And Now, Some Words from the President . . .

As a postscript on what will hopefully be yet another four-and-out-the-door GOP president, here is a collection of quotes from King George II. Yes, George "Dubya" Bush, *He bugs Gore*, the crowned prince of Kennebunkport, a graduate of Yale *and* Harvard, a governor, owner of a Major League Baseball team, and corporate executive. A man who once flew fighter planes. A man who nearly died at the hands of a pretzel. A man who has the ability to push the button on his own weapons of mass destruction. A real blue-blooded, dyed-in-the-wool American hero.

Reminder: These are not anagrams, nor are they French phrases. This is the forty-third president of the United States of America making the best use of English he possibly can.

- "They misunderestimated me."
- "The grown-ups are back in charge."
- "I know how hard it is for you to put food on your families."
- "If we don't stop extending our troops all around the world in nation-building missions, then we're going to have a serious problem coming down the road. And I'm going to prevent that."
- "Rarely is the question asked: Is our children learning?"
- "As you know, these are open forums. You're able to come and listen to what I have to say."
- "First, let me make it very clear, poor people aren't necessarily killers. Just because you happen to be not rich doesn't mean you're willing to kill."
- "I'm a patient man. And when I say I'm a patient man, I mean I'm a patient man."
- "The problem with the French is that they don't have a word for entrepreneur."
- "It's amazing I won. I was running against peace, prosperity, and incumbency."
- "In other words, I don't think people ought to be compelled to make the decision which they think is best for their family."
- "See, free nations are peaceful nations. Free nations don't attack each other. Free nations don't develop weapons of mass destruction."
- "I glance at the headlines just to kind of get a flavor for what's moving. I rarely read the stories, and get briefed by people who probably read the news themselves."

- "There's an old saying in Tennessee—I know it's in Texas, probably in Tennessee—that says, fool me once, shame on—shame on you. Fool me—you can't get fooled again."
- "We've got pockets of persistent poverty in our society, which I refuse to declare defeat—I mean, I refuse to allow them to continue on. And so one of the things that we're trying to do is to encourage a faith-based initiative to spread its wings all across America, to be able to capture this great compassionate spirit."
- "I think we agree, the past is over."

If King George II was really up on his American history, if he was really down with his Bible, he'd know that a sentence divided against itself cannot stand . . .

135

Deference to the religious right had become a central tenet of Republicanism since the 1960s, and with it came a reliance on governmental power that would have been anathema if applied to economic activities.
—Lewis L. Gould

Chapter Thirteen

Adam in the Garden:
Thursday

"Hello, Tom."

"I prayed for you last night, Adam."

"That's the nicest thing you can do for a person, but the most condescending thing you can tell them."

"Well, then . . . Sounds like you don't need me to look out for you anymore. You must have some faith."

"Tom, I've got faith in God, but I've also got faith in Einstein and Dean Kamer and all of those cancer, AIDS, and stem cell researchers. I trust them and want them looking out for me. They've saved a lot more lives than your brand of pay-to-pray religion."

> May we never confuse
> honest dissent with
> disloyal subversion.
> —Dwight D.
> Eisenhower

"Somebody's coming out swingin' today. Slow down, Apple Cart. You bring your wallet?"

"Yep."

"Good. You forgot to leave that money again yesterday, you know."

"I know. And I *confess* . . . I forgot on purpose. Both days."

"What?!"

"And here's another confession. I was only pulling your leg yesterday. I'm not gay. In fact, I have a girlfriend back home."

"Why? Why did you lie to a man of the cloth, Adam?"

"I just get a kick out of people getting all high and mighty."

"Ha! This city has ruined you. May the good Lord save your soul."

138

"I'll tell you something else I thought of, Tom. . . I'm tired of oxymorons like compassionate conservative. All Bush knows about that is how to *conserve* his *compassion*."

"Very clever, my little Miss Guided Youth."

"Tom, that's almost as patronizing as telling me I need to be prayed for. Look, I've got some living to do before I can even consider buying what you're selling. And the way I see it is, I'll get to live a full life before I settle down like the rest of you Born-Again Republicans."

"You're as deep as a kiddie pool."

"From being condescending in a passive aggressive way to being outspokenly condescending . . . That'll convince me."

"Why did you come today, Adam? What can I do for you and your made-up mind?"

"Here's my confession. It's my list, like your list from Tuesday . . . I confess, I once lied about breaking the neighbor's window.

Worst part was, I said my little brother threw the ball. The next day I admitted to it."

"See? You're why we need the death penalty. Ha!"

"Funny, Tom. Always funny. Speaking of breaking, the list goes on. I broke teeth on frozen Charleston Chews when I was a kid. Three different times."

"Blasphemy."

"I just couldn't kick the habit. You'll like this one, too. I'm such a bad boy that when Evie said 'No' on prom night, I didn't push it. I was willing to wait for her."

"Saint Apple Cart."

"And in college, I volunteered as a candy striper."

"Stripper?"

"Striper. At the hospital. On the oncology floor. I only missed three classes in college and that was because my grandmother passed away. I was christened and I was confirmed. I always took out the trash and I never used the Lord's name in vain. When I was little and had a paper route, I never, ever skimmed off the top. I don't need Mel Gibson to tell me to take my sins seriously because unlike him and you and George Bush, I don't have a closet full of sins! I have nothing to be ashamed of. At the same time, I haven't seen enough of this world. I'm ready to test the waters."

"Careful you don't drown, Apple Cart."

"You came out all right, didn't you?"

"More or less. I'm sure the trail you'll leave won't be quite as wide as mine. Just beware the scorched earth policy."

"Sounds funny coming from a Republican. All right, enough of this charade. I have a favor to ask. Can we just talk? Step outside of this

> Confession of our faults is the next thing to innocency.
> —Publius Syrus

139

stupid booth and talk before I go? This confessional is a bit ridiculous. I mean, it's made of the boards from the hockey rink!"

"So that's what it is. I've been wondering. But sure. Let's meet face-to-face. And actually, can we step out to Seventh Avenue? I need a butt. You going to start smoking now, too?"

"Nope."

"Ah, you *are* a master of avoiding temptation."

"That's me. You look older than I thought, Tom . . . Fifty-three?"

"Cute, Apple Cart. Forty-five is more like it. Nice to finally meet you."

"Nice to meet you, too. So, even more than living a full life, my decision is based on what I can stomach and what I can't. It's all of these people spouting off about what's right and wrong with everything from homosexuality to abortion to stem cell research to deficit spending to separation of church and state to privatizing public education."

"Yeah, public money for private schools is a load of crap. I'm a product of the public schools."

"Well, if that isn't an argument for a bigger education budget, I don't know what is!"

"Get a loada you, Apple Cart. Sense of humor and everything! You sure you want to turn your back on the GOP? What about your old man?"

"I'm going to have a family soon and I think I need to think more about that than my father. And who knows, if I play my cards right I might just be able to have my cake and eat it, too."

> I do not know which makes
> a man more conservative—
> to know nothing but
> the present, or nothing
> but the past.
> —John Maynard Keynes

Is there a solution to any of this, then? Yes, actually. What needs to be done, clearly, is to give every one of the pro-life activists diseases that cause their lungs, liver, and kidneys to fail. Faced with their own imminent mortality, it's a safe bet many of them will take the time to seriously reappraise their stance on stem cells . . .
—J. Pinkerton

"Dubya's the wedding cake, kid. And the Democrats are a stale cookie on the buffet table. I know he wasn't perfect his first four years, but Bush has got experience now. He's the only hope we've got."

"I don't know about that. I may be from the sticks, but I know what city life will be like after he's through slashing funds. Lots and lots of crime. No education and no rehabilitation. Just incarceration."

"You rap now?"

"Just an unintentional Dirty South kind of a rhyme."

"Eminem beware."

"Nobody in the GOP is looking out for poor minorities, immigrants included. I mean, just this morning I watched a teleconference . . . Clarence Thomas phoned in from Washington and spoke with Condi Rice and Colin Powell and I've never seen such a thing. Even though there were like two hundred of us watching, they were telling Al Sharpton jokes. Actually, I think they were doing it *because* we were watching."

"Remember any of the jokes? I'm looking for some new material."

Clarence Thomas is my color, but he's not my kind. Do not confuse black leaders with leading blacks. Condoleezza Rice, Colin Powell, and Clarence Thomas don't lead anybody.
—Al Sharpton, on *Hardball with Chris Matthews*

"Sorry."

"So, what else?"

"Just the same old point about homosexuality. I don't know why I keep going back to it. Maybe it's because I'm amazed; we've got people dying in the Middle East, people dying in our own country because the health care system is so screwed up, and gay marriage is worth worrying about?"

"Adam, I don't understand why you'll listen to all these odd-balls, but you won't trust me, an ordained minister. Isn't it time you grew up and acted like a man? Put these questions to rest and pledge yourself to the party of freedom, the party that allows you to be all that you can be. The party that refuses to compromise its ethics and morals, and that holds accountability near and dear to its heart! Praise Jesus!"

"Look at this building, Tom. The Garden. The world's most famous arena. What a perfect choice for the Republican convention: tons of money flying around and no results. They've got the highest payroll in hockey and haven't made the playoffs in years . . . And the Knicks couldn't beat the University of Montana right now. No championships since the days of Bill Bradley . . . Lots of talk, lots of cash, but no accountability. A perfect backdrop for Dubya."

"The Rangers put a flashy All-Star team on the ice every night and the Knicks have brought Marbury home. I love what happens in this building and I especially love what's gone on in here this week."

"You don't even believe what you're saying, Tom."

"Not really. But I'm a diehard fan, you know? Speaking of which, you sure you don't want to stick around for the speeches tonight? Should be pretty inspirational."

"I'm going to pass. At this point, I don't need my politics to be determined by a party, just like I don't need to have confession with another person. I like it better when it is just me and my God, nobody else to screw it up. No offense, of course."

"None taken. Okay, it's time for the air conditioning and those speeches. That'll be forty dollars, please."

"I spent it all. On bagels and a Metro Pass. On falafel and cover charges. On having fun, just like you suggested."

"Well, at least it went to something good. You oughta be proud, Apple Cart. You can tell your friends you survived the Garden with your values intact. You gave not in to temptation."

"Yay for me."

"You'll have to change your name now, you know."

"Maybe to Mark?"

"Who's Mark?"

I really believe that the pagans, and the abortionists, and the feminists, and the gays and the lesbians who are actively trying to make that an alternative lifestyle, the ACLU, People For the American Way, all of them who have tried to secularize America—I point the finger in their face and say you helped this happen.
—Jerry Falwell,
referring to 9/11 on *The 700 Club*

"It's hard to tell when you're being legitimate. No wonder the Republicans like you so much. Okay, I need to run and so do you. Goodbye, Tom."

"Twenty dollars?"

"Take care."

"Ten dollars?"

"Peace."

Dear Journal,

I feel good tonight. I am excited to get back to Evie and to talk to my folks. I know that I'll be letting Dad down, but I can live with that, especially since I think he'll come around. I don't think the news will be that big of a deal for Mom. She's cool like that.

I was impressed, this week, by St. Pat's, but it was St. John the Divine that really blew me away. All of the churches within the cathedral, it was mind boggling. I think it is the world's biggest. I felt like such a city boy taking the subway up there. But my favorite church, by far, was St. Paul's. It's the city's oldest church, built in 1766. It used to sit in the shadow of the Twin Towers, but even before September 11th it was an amazing place. George Washington prayed there for his first two years as president, and the Frenchman who designed the layout for Washington, D.C., helped design part of its altar.

When the Twin Towers came down, not one window was broken. I know divine intervention when I see it.

I mention these churches because, just like there's something for everyone in New York eating-wise and entertainment-wise and work-wise, there's something for everyone church-wise. St. Paul's is an Episcopal Church and I can see myself attending. It's a place I could call home.

New York has been so good to me and I know I'll be back. There isn't much for me in Montana and Evie wants to live in a city. I think we'll love it here once all these Republicans are gone! I admit, at times I felt anger in my heart. The delegates at this convention, I can hear them all saying, "I will pray for you." What they mean to say is they will do all they can to convert you and to save your lost soul. They're all like smug, preachy robots dressed in navy blue. Not what God had in mind, I suspect.

So, I think that tomorrow I will get to work on becoming a full-time New Yorker. And after that, who knows, maybe even a Democrat! I'm not sure yet. I just know I'll be writing to you again. I look forward to it. All of it.

Regard not the particular sect or denomination of the candidate—look to his character.
—Noah Webster

Chapter Fourteen

The Same Ol' Grand Old Party

The problems with the GOP don't begin with King George II and they certainly don't end with him. We should be so lucky. For the entire 150-year history of the GOP, save maybe those first few Honest Abe "a house divided" years, the problems have basically been the same. Let's see what the future holds for the GOP.

In the coming months, judgment will be passed on several key figures, among them my very own governor, John Rowland.[55] Impeachment looms as all of his fellow GOPers have jumped ship. The last anyone heard from Patty Rowland (*want yard plot!!!*), she was mocking *The Hartford Courant* for being so mean to her husband

---

[55] Contractors who worked, *gratis*, on his cabin received multimillion-dollar state contracts. Under Rowland, the state also lost millions to Enron, fell for the Patriots ploy of building a stadium in Hartford, and then gave UConn a stadium just in time for the Big East to become a glorified Pop Warner league.

> His habitual
> violation of traffic
> laws finally caught
> up with him.
> —Joan Claybrook,
> on Bill Janklow

with a catty version of "The Night Before Christmas." Since that time, I believe she's been soaking her head in the hot tub at the cabin in question. Ho, ho, ho.

Bill Janklow has already received his sentence, although it is the lightest of slaps on his fat-cat wrist. Janklow was charged with second-degree manslaughter, reckless driving, speeding, and failure to stop at a stop sign, and could have received ten years in prison as well as $10,000 in fines. He killed a man, and even the most cynical of cynics expected him to feel the full wrath of the law. Instead, he was given one hundred days in jail. One hundred days . . .

If he was a black man living in Illinois, he'd be six feet under by now.

I am also curious to see where U.S. Attorney General John Ashcroft ends up. When the war in Iraq comes to a close—I can't say "end" because according to King George II, it's already long over—and the U.S. economy recovers, calmer heads will prevail. I think that, more likely than not, Ashcroft will find himself teaching at Bob Jones University. Either that, or president of an anti-fan club—Johnny Depp, Michael Moore, Susan Sarandon, Ellen DeGeneres, Al Sharpton—take your pick. Maybe Rush Limbaugh can be his anti-fan club vice president.

Former Tyco exec Dennis Kozlowski will receive his jail sentence shortly. I hope his legal fees far surpass the $2 million that was spent on his wife's bacchanalian birthday bash in Italy, approximately half of which was paid for by Tyco. Kozlowski and Tyco

> He's not much of
> an attorney and I
> know for sure he's
> not a general.
> —Wesley Clark,
> on John Ashcroft

both contribute to the GOP, of course. How else can you maintain a life of togas, bacchanalia, and bustiness?

Speaking of the courts, the Supreme Court will present a problem for years to come. Watch as issues of civil rights becomes less than civil and watch as the separation of church and state slowly but surely becomes less separate than originally intended. Although there are several key justices to worry about, it is Antonin Scalia I fear the most. He was so cute in those Prince Spaghetti commercials, his grandmother leaning out of the window every Wednesday, up there in the North End of Boston, and calling him in for dinner. What happened? Now he's looking to return the U.S. to the conservatism of The Gilded Age. Does he really want to see the gospel-singing Hardings reincarnated? It's time he got used to rappers like Warren G and all the rest kickin' it live in the Dirty South. It's time he resigned himself to women capable of doing more than serving up martinis.

Maybe Justice Scalia needs a night out with Snoop Dogg. I have no doubt it would be more fun than a hunting trip with Dick Cheney. Snoop doesn't need any mechanical help to keep his heart beating; no little purple pill to *shnizzle* the *vizzle*. *Girls Gone Wild*

He's so Old School, he's Old Testament, misty over the era when military institutes did not have to accept women, when elite schools did not have to make special efforts with blacks, when a gay couple in their own bedroom could be clapped in irons, when women were packed off to Our Lady of Perpetual Abstinence Home for Unwed Mothers. He's an American archetype, or Archie type.
—Maureen Dowd, on Antonin Scalia

might be just what Dr. Anal Orange ordered. More medicinal than that martini!

And of course, there's everybody's favorite: Conan the Barbarian. I would be lying if I said there isn't a little part of me that gets a kick out of seeing Arnold Schwarzenegger in the governor's office. It would seem his barbarian days are far behind him now. His sword-swinging, couple-swinging, ass-grabbing, steroids-and-pot days stacked neat and clean in his closet.[56]

And if there's anyone out there who doesn't believe that people start to look alike after years of marriage, just check out the plate tectonics of Maria Shriver's face. She is becoming more eastern European with each passing day. But Californians know that she's their only hope. If Maria can look more and more like him, maybe he will think more and more like Maria. Maybe?

Schwarzenegger (*Czar Egg Her News*, in tribute to Maria's former career) is lying low as he deals with everything from debt to immigration to San Francisco's embracing of gay marriage.

Friends, family, countrymen, wife . . . you deserve this. The Up With People think tank is proud to present the governor of California, Arnold Schwarzenegger, and his backup singers, The Arnettes!

(Stage Directions: Applause!)

The governor asked me to give him the opportunity, before tying up this book, to apologize for all of his groping, womanizing ways. Governor Schwarzenegger, it's all yours . . .

(Stage Directions: The Arnettes join in wherever you see the *italics*.)

"A lot you see in stories / is not true. A lot you see in stories / *Is not true*. But I have to tell you / wherever der is smoke, der's fire. That is true / *That is true*."

150

---

[56] Interesting that the steroids situation that King George II suddenly cares so much about will be coming to a head in Arnie's state . . .

"Let me tell you something / tell you something."

"So I wan' to say to you / Yes, I have behave badly. Yes, it's true / *Yes, it's true.* I was on movie sets / And I've done things dat were not right. Not right / *No, not right.*"

"Let me tell you something / tell you something."

"I t'ought dat it was playful / But I recognize I've offended. And to all dat I've offended / *To all that I've offended.* I wan' to say I'm sorry / deeply sorry / *Deeply sorry.*"

"Let me tell you something / tell you something."

"I apologize, I'm sorry / Cuz dis is not what I wan' to do. *Want to do / Want to do.* No, it's not what I wan' to do / Want to do / *Want to do.*"

His voice lifts in falsetto sincerity, a hand rising with it. Maria's eyes gaze skyward, following this moving monument, five digits born in a foreign land but digging deeply into the American firmament. He is her Horatio Algier. Her Sonny Bono.

(Stage direction: The Arnettes bow their heads in deference.)

"As duh governor / I wan' to do / I wan' to do . . . As duh governor / I wan' to prove to womens / prove to duh womens dat I will be a champion / a champion for duh womens everywhere. *Duh womens / Duh womens.*"

"That I will be a champion . . ."

The hand drops, the well-coiffed heads behind him raise. There is one big finish coming our way, folks!

". . . A champion for duh womens / *A champion for women.* And I hope dat you will give me / *Hope that you will give me* / The chance to prove dat I / I / I / I am a champion for duh womens."

"Let me tell you something! / tell you something! / tell you something!"

The kettle drummer slows the pace for the jazzy-bluesy, bring-it-on-home finish, Arnold dropping to a knee and waving his top hat in Mammy, Mammy, Mammy style.

"Now let's."

"*Yes, let's.*"

"Oh yes, let's."

"*Oh yes, let's.*"

"Get back / *oh back* / back / *yes back* / back to duh future of California."

"*Cal-i-for-ni-a . . .*"

"Cal-i-for-ni-aaaaaaaaaaaaaaaaaaaa. Cha!!!"

And the crowd goes wild, women rejoicing in a wave of wet forgiveness, the Earth, or at least the thirty-first state, saved for one more day.

And a new star is born for the Grand Old Party. Cha.

My attitude about all that has changed radically.
I used to feel that women were here for
one reason. Sex was simply another kind of
exercise, another body function.
—Arnold Schwarzenegger

Money is human happiness in the abstract: he, then, who is no longer capable of enjoying human happiness in the concrete, devotes his heart entirely to money.
—Arthur Schopenhauer

Republicans get elected as a knee-jerk reaction. We get ticked off about losing our jobs and we fear for our lives. We believe a rebate will boost our fortunes and that a billion-dollar hike in defense spending will make our homes safer; meanwhile, we forget that high school dropouts tend to turn criminal and that the GOP agenda doesn't include money enough to rehabilitate them. Reaganesque amnesia sets in as we forget all of this in a fit of hope for our financial future. After two or three years we are reminded, though, and yet another Republican president succumbs to the four-and-out-the-door syndrome.

American democracy is just like organized religion. There is an amazing potential to do good. Both are capable of setting a wonderful example, of modeling how life should be lived. It's the conservative agenda that sours everything. Scare tactics, passing judgment, personal gain at public expense. A Republican system with Democratic ideals is our greatest hope just so long as the original intentions are not forgotten in a fit of Alzheimer's, à la *Dr. Anal Orange*. It is love and not fear, empathy and not greed, that makes a house a home.

King George II has somehow managed to inject his sourness into our home. His right-wing religion is making a mockery of both church and state. Enron's organizational culture was exemplified by corporate centerfolds and scare tactics to sell insurance. King George II's corporate culture is one of extreme nationalism and a strict constructionist's view of the Bible. Every day is Sunday for our president. Before his midlife crisis, *he* was in peril. Ever since, it has been the United States that has suffered.

Shame on us for putting stock into his kind of shock value. Shame on us for risking so much just to get a $300 rebate.[57] Shame on us for ever thinking that America would benefit from a "moronarchy" like the First Family Bush.

Let's not be too hard on ourselves, though. Fact finding can be difficult when a multimillion-dollar war chest is being put to use. Even the savviest can be duped. I myself have never voted Republican, but for those of you out there who have, don't feel too bad. Just don't do it again. Please.

Fortunately, the tides have turned. When I first wrote "Bible thumping," things were not looking good for America. Our soldiers were dying at a rate of more than one per day, news of "economic growth" was more contrived than a Dennis Miller punch line, and Operation Distraction was quite the success, as the GOP diverted the nation's eyes to Mars, steroids in baseball, and gay marriage. The worst part was, there appeared to be nobody out there who could de-

---

[57] I knocked my credit card debt down from $5,000 to $4,700. A tremendous boost to our economy, for sure.

throne King George II. The Democrats were dangerously close to becoming yet another Know Nothing Party. They had to come up with something and quick.

They may have found their man now. But just to be sure, they'd better come prepared with the proper tools and a whole lot of elbow grease. The way our national debt is ballooning, the way Iraq and Afghanistan are unraveling, the way our schools are hurting; health care; Social Security; NAFTA . . . America is a handyman's special in need of some serious work: loving care and top-notch repair.

> The combination of being a Republican, of being an emperor, a Texan, and outspoken is really a bad mix . . . Let's face it, who likes an empire?
> —Jose Maria Aznar, Spanish prime minister

In laying the foundation for our nation, the forefathers squared off on many a divisive issue. The Democratic Party grew out of one such debate as Hamilton and Jefferson argued the pros and cons of federalism. The ultimate test, however, was not the ratification of the Constitution, as many thought it would be. No, it was the Civil War. And again, after all was said and done and the Constitution had been amended, everybody was fooled into thinking the nation had passed the test. But here we are, more than one hundred and fifty years later, and still we can't resolve the race issue. With that in mind, ask yourself this: How quickly can we expect to bring three diverse religions together in Iraq? Here at home, we have yet to get even a 55 percent on the equality test. We are still empowering leaders who treat human beings as less than human. We still have a tendency to be penny-wise and pound-foolish when it comes to electing public officials.

Friends, family, countrymen, wife . . . we don't need to encourage the GOP any more than they encourage themselves, and we certainly don't need to see more of the First Family in Washington, D.C., either. Not if we want a White House that feels more like a home.

Taxes are the price of civilization.
—Oliver Wendell Holmes Jr.,
U.S. Supreme Court Justice

Bibliography

The Columbia Encyclopedia: Sixth Edition. Edited by Paul Lagassé. New York: Columbia University Press, 2003.

The Dictionary of Cultural Literacy. Edited by E. D. Hirsch Jr., Joseph F. Kett, and James Trefil. Boston: Houghton Mifflin Company, 1991.

The International Dictionary of Thoughts. Compiled by John P. Bradley, Leo F. Daniels, and Thomas C. Jones. Chicago: J.G. Ferguson Publishing Company, 1969.

http://www.mbhs.edu/~bconnell/anagrams.shtml (*Brendan's Online Anagrams*)

The New Dictionary of Thoughts. Compiled by Tryon Edwards. New York: StanBook Incorporated, 1977.

O'Brien, Cormac. *Secret Lives of the U.S. Presidents.* Philadelphia: Quirk Books, 2004.

The Quotable Politician. Edited by William B. Whitman. Guilford, Connecticut: The Lyons Press, 2003.

www.slate.com

Toole, John Kennedy. *A Confederacy of Dunces.* New York: Grove Press, 1980.

Uncle John's Giant 10th Anniversary Bathroom Reader. Ashland, Oregon: Bathroom Readers' Press, 1997.

Webster's New World Dictionary of American English: Third College Edition. Edited by Victoria Neufeldt. Cleveland and New York: Webster's New World, 1988.

Witcover, Jules. *Party of the People: A History of the Democrats.* New York: Random House, 2003.

Zinn, Howard. *A People's History of the United States: 1492–Present.* New York: Perennial Classics, 2001.

My gratitude to George Donahue. It's nice when an editor need not be acknowledged with a concession speech!

My thanks to Sally and Dave Howe for a liberal education that included showing me how to make a house a home.

And finally, all the hugs in the world to Alicia and Noelle Solís. You both epitomize hate's opposite and no written word could ever express the depths of my affection.

163

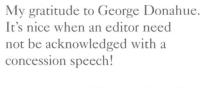

About the Author

Randy Howe is a registered Independent who chooses his poker and golf buddies by how qualified they are and not according to political affiliation. He lives in Connecticut with his conservative wife and liberal daughter, a cat that could care less, and a dog that will vote for whomever leaves the lid off the trash. He is the author of *Flags of the Fifty States and Their Incredible Histories* and *The Quotable Teacher*, and—in a nod to impartiality—*Why I Hate the Democrats*.

In this world of sin and sorrow there is always something to be thankful for; as for me, I rejoice that I am not a Republican.
—H. L. Mencken

If a conservative is a liberal who has been mugged . . . A liberal is a conservative who realizes that she can't have what's being conserved.
—Debra J. Dickerson

Our responsibility as privileged human beings is to pay back for the opportunities we've received.
—Kathryn Anastos